My Best Wishes,

[signature]

2008

Dear Mark,

Pursue righteousness and a godly life, along with faith, love, perseverance and gentleness. 1 Tim 6:11 on your 59th birthday

Love
Mom & Dad

Praise for

The Pursuit

Pat Williams is one of the most positive, energetic, successful people I know. Businessman, motivator, author, father of 19—how does he do it all and do it so well? At last, he shares his secrets in *The Pursuit*. Absorb the wisdom within these pages and live intentionally, because dreams really *do* come true!

Terry Meeuwsen
Co-host, *The 700 Club*

I have known Pat Williams for 25 years. I have enjoyed his many books and find them insightful, humorous and always thought provoking. Pat Williams is one of the brightest minds in our professional sports executive world.

Carl Peterson
President, General Manager and CEO, Kansas City Chiefs

As the chair of the DeVos Sport Business Management Graduate Program at the University of Central Florida, one of my top 10 things to do each year is make sure Pat Williams speaks to the DeVos students. The reason is simple: In 30 minutes, he packs in more wisdom to guide their lives than anyone I know. He has given the gift of that wisdom in this wonderful new book.

Dr. Richard Lapchick
Chair, DeVos Sport Business Management Program at UCF
Director, Institute for Diversity and Ethics in Sport
Director, National Consortium for Academics and Sports

Few people have studied success and successful people as Pat Williams has. Even fewer have been able to take what they have learned and apply it to their own pursuit. Pat's life of adventure and success is a testament that the principles he lays out in *The Pursuit* can change your life!

Stan Van Gundy
Head Coach, Orlando Magic

Wow, what a wonderful read! This book is a treasure chest of wisdom filled with advice, stories and anecdotes that will impact your journey through life in the most positive of ways! This book will change your life.

Deb Patterson
Head Women's Basketball Coach, Kansas State University

The Pursuit is a valuable new book from my friend Pat Williams. It is packed with wisdom for people of all ages and will serve as a road map for years to come. I want all my players to read it.

Sue Semrau
Head Women's Basketball Coach, Florida State University

WISDOM *for the*

ADVENTURE

of YOUR LIFE

The PURSUIT

PAT WILLIAMS
with JIM DENNEY

Regal

From Gospel Light
Ventura, California, U.S.A.

Published by Regal
From Gospel Light
Ventura, California, U.S.A.
www.regalbooks.com
Printed in the U.S.A.

Library of Congress Cataloging-in-Publication Data
Williams, Pat, 1940-
  The pursuit : wisdom for the adventure of your life / Pat Williams with Jim Denney.
    p. cm.
  ISBN 978-0-8307-4599-9 (hard cover)
  1. Success. 2. Conduct of life. 3. Williams, Pat, 1940- 4. Christian life. I. Denney, James D. II. Title.
  BF637.S8W52135 2008
  158.1—dc22

                                                                    2007037740

      1   2   3   4   5   6   7   8   9   10   /   11   10   09   08

Rights for publishing this book outside the U.S.A. or in non-English languages are administered by Gospel Light Worldwide, an international not-for-profit ministry. For additional information, please visit www.glww.org, email info@glww.org, or write to Gospel Light Worldwide, 1957 Eastman Avenue, Ventura, CA 93003, U.S.A.

*This book is dedicated
to Jim Henry and David Uth,
two men of wisdom who live
The Pursuit every day.*

Contents

First Word: Feasting on Life 8

1. Control What You Can 16
   (Let Go of Everything Else)

2. Be Patient 47

3. Pay Your Dues 72
   (You Need to Have Experience)

4. Keep It Simple 93

5. Don't Run from Your Problems 113
   (They Give You an Opportunity to Sell Yourself to Others)

6. Pay Attention to the Little Things 137

7. The Pursuit of Wisdom 159

8. The Mindset of a Learner 170

Last Word: A Gift from Karyn 198

Endnotes 200

Feasting on Life

Let's face it: I've got kids who are probably older than you.

But I remember what it was like to be where you are in life. Oh yes, my friend, I remember it like it was just this morning.

For some, it happens right after high school, for others, a bit later. For me, I was in my twenties, with my school years behind me and my adult life yet to come. I had dreams—big dreams. And I had a passion for living each day to the absolute max—feasting on life, sucking the marrow out of every moment, and pursuing my dreams.

And I'll tell you something: Most of my youthful dreams have come true! I have lived—and I'm still living—an absolutely amazing life.

I have traveled the world. I've known sports stars, celebrities and presidents. I have known the thrill of a world championship victory. I have taken part in accomplishments (such as founding the Orlando Magic in 1987) that I never even imagined when I was your age. Awesome, unbelievable things have happened in my life—and for a very good reason.

When I was beginning my pursuit, I received some good advice from a wise man. I followed his advice and based my career on it—and that has made all the difference in my life.

Now I want to share that advice with you. I want you to have the kind of amazing, fulfilling, exciting life I'm having. I want to pass along to you the wisdom I received when I was where you are in life. I'm going to show you how to live with the same sense of excitement and adventure that I've known.

Let me introduce you to the man whose wisdom changed my life.

"You'll Never Meet Another Man Like My Husband"

My days as a minor league catcher in the Philadelphia Phillies organization were over. The top brass had watched me play for two seasons, 1962 to 1963, and they let me know that I was in the twilight of a mediocre playing career. Clay Dennis, the Phillies farm director, told me there were two general manager posts open within the system. One was in Bakersfield, California; the other was in Spartanburg, South Carolina. Clay offered the jobs to me and another former player, Dick Smith.

I asked Dick, "Which do you want? Spartanburg or Bakersfield?"

"Doesn't matter to me," Dick said. "You pick."

"Okay," I said. "I'll take Spartanburg."

I had gone to Wake Forest University, about 150 miles from Spartanburg, and my dad's family was spread across the Carolinas. So I had ties to the area. I thought Spartanburg was my best bet—but I had no idea what a life-changing decision that would turn out to be.

Clay told me, "First thing you do when you get to Spartanburg is look up Mr. R. E. Littlejohn. He's one of the owners, and he'll be your key guy."

So I loaded everything I owned into my car and headed for my first real job. I remember that drive like it was yesterday. I arrived on a cold, rainy Sunday in February 1965, and found Mr. Littlejohn's home at 315 Glendalyn Place.

When I knocked on the door, it was about two in the afternoon. I was so nervous at the thought of meeting my new boss that my heart was pounding like a jackhammer against my ribcage.

Mrs. Littlejohn answered the door. Though her name was Marion, I soon learned that everyone called her Sam.

"Hi, I'm Pat Williams," I said. "I'm the new general manager of the Spartanburg Phillies."

She greeted me warmly and invited me in. "I'm sorry my husband isn't home," she said. "He was called out of town for a funeral." She offered me refreshments, and we chatted for a few minutes.

Finally, when I got up to leave, Mrs. Littlejohn said the most amazing thing: "No matter how long you're in ball"—that's what she called baseball—"you'll never meet another man like my husband."

I didn't know what to make of that statement, but I was soon to find out that Mrs. Littlejohn's words were not empty hyperbole. She was right. In all the years that I've been in "ball," both baseball and basketball, I have never met anyone like Mr. R. E. Littlejohn.

A Quest for Wisdom

His given name was Richard Erlic Littlejohn, and though most people called him "Mr. R. E.," I usually called him "Coach," because that was the role he played in my life. In addition to being a co-owner of a Phillies farm system team, he was a successful petroleum carrier executive, and I met him for the first time in his office. I found him to be impressive without being the least imposing or intimidating.

Mr. R. E. was a courteous, soft-spoken Southern gentleman with a gift for putting people at ease. When you met him, he looked you in the eye and took a genuine interest in you. In all the years I knew him, I never once heard him utter a cross or sarcastic word. He never swore. He never showed impatience with anyone. I never heard him speak an unkind word about anyone—not even about those who were unkind to him.

The man was as unforgettable as his wife had described him, only more so. I couldn't put my finger on just what it was that so struck me about the man, but whatever it was, I was intrigued. I ran the Spartanburg team for four years, from 1965 to 1968, and Mr. R. E. became my mentor, coach, encourager and best friend. From him, I learned everything I needed to know about how to have a life of meaning, purpose and true success.

Looking back over more than four decades in the sports business, I can see that every good thing that has happened to me in my career and my life is a direct result of the lessons I learned from this man.

Mr. R. E. possessed a wonderful quality called *wisdom*—and he had it in abundance. He was both outwardly and inwardly successful. He reaped the rewards of material success, yet he also possessed true spiritual contentment and a rich family life. Ralph Waldo Emerson once wrote, "Raphael paints wisdom; Handel sings it, Phidias carves it, Shakespeare writes it, Wren builds it, Columbus sails it, Luther preaches it, Washington arms it, Watt mechanizes it." Emerson could have added, "Mr. R. E. Littlejohn lives it."

From watching his life, I learned the difference between knowledge and wisdom. I learned that knowledge likes to speak; wisdom prefers to listen. Knowledge takes things apart; wisdom put things back together. Knowledge prides itself on its achievements; wisdom humbly thirsts to learn more. Every day I spent with him, Mr. R. E. taught me by his example the truth of the ancient words "Wisdom is supreme; therefore get wisdom. Though it cost all you have, get understanding" (Prov. 4:7). As I have looked around this world, I have seen many smart, educated, knowledgeable people—but very few who are wise.

When I started working for Mr. R. E., I was the youngest and greenest general manager in history. Over the next four years, I had countless visits with him in his home, his office and over lunch. With each of those encounters, I became infused with just a little more of Mr. Littlejohn's wisdom.

I left Spartanburg after the 1968 baseball season to start my career in the National Basketball Association. From the time I left Spartanburg until the day Mr. Littlejohn passed away in 1987, I never made a career move or any other significant decision without seeking his wisdom. I would call him from Philadelphia, Chicago, Atlanta or wherever I happened to be, and ask his advice.

Not only was Mr. Littlejohn a mentor to me, but there were also countless people of all ages, in all walks of life, who sought wisdom and counsel from this remarkable man. College presidents, educators, pastors, coaches, corporate CEOs, bankers and students continually went to him for advice. Mr. Littlejohn was not a formally educated man. He spent two years at Furman University in Greenville before entering the business world. Yet he was so richly imbued with wisdom that people sought him out from near and far.

The Pursuit

In recent years, I've become a mentor to others, just as Mr. Littlejohn was to me. Hardly a day goes by that I don't receive a visit, phone call or email from a young person asking my advice. More often than not, the advice I give is almost word for word what Mr. Littlejohn imparted to me, because the wisdom he shared with me when I was in my twenties is just as valid today.

I have distilled the most important lessons I learned from Mr. Littlejohn into six key wisdom principles:

1. Control what you can (let go of everything else).
2. Be patient.
3. Pay your dues (you need to have experience).
4. Keep it simple.
5. Don't run from your problems (they give you an opportunity to sell yourself to others).
6. Pay attention to the little things.

Mr. Littlejohn took the time to implant his wisdom in me. There was no formal classroom setting in which he lectured me on wisdom. Rather, he imparted his insights in the flow of everyday life. Whenever a situation came up where there was a lesson to be learned, he would take the time to underscore that lesson. He'd tell me stories from his own experience or pass along some life principle. He taught me to see all of life as a quest for wisdom.

When I began my apprenticeship under Mr. Littlejohn, I was 24 years old and intensely ambitious. Mr. Littlejohn saw how eager and hungry I was to succeed. He saw that I was goal-oriented, focused and relentlessly driven to reach my full potential. He knew that I desperately wanted to jump right into what I call "The Pursuit," the headlong quest for the adventure of life.

But over the years, Mr. Littlejohn had seen many promising, highly motivated young people like me. He had seen many of them start strong only to fall by the wayside. In spite of all their ambition and lofty goals, they failed to reach their potential. Mr. Littlejohn had already negotiated the tricky passages of life that I wasn't even aware of. He knew what I needed to learn in order to finish strong and win the race.

I was an apt (and rapt) student, and I absorbed everything he taught me. I have tested and proven these principles in the trials of my own life, and I truly wouldn't be where I am today if these principles didn't work.

These six keys to mastering the adventure of life—and the life of adventure—are the very principles I have been passing along to my 19 children, to the young people in our Orlando Magic organization and to the young audiences I often speak to. One of the most important things I do as a father, business leader and author is to pour into the next generation the rich and life-changing truths that Mr. Littlejohn so generously poured into me.

I truly look at my life as consisting of two stages. Stage One was the first 24 years of my life, which I call "The Preparation." Stage Two is my life since meeting Mr. R. E.

Littlejohn, which I call "The Pursuit." It was only after I came under his mentorship that I truly understood what the adventure of life was all about.

There are not enough days in one lifetime to sit down and individually mentor every young person I come in contact with. But through this book, I hope to launch thousands of young people on their own Pursuit. And when I say that, I'm looking right at *you*.

So pull up a chair, my friend. Let me share with you the wisdom that my mentor, Mr. Littlejohn, poured into me. Let these truths seep into your soul and saturate every fiber of your being. Get ready for the adventure of a lifetime. Prepare yourself for The Pursuit.

Your life is about to change.

Chapter 1

Control What You Can
(Let Go of Everything Else)

In 1962, at the end of my senior year at Wake Forest University, my teammates and I skipped the commencement exercises so that we could play in the NCAA regional baseball tournament in Gastonia, North Carolina. Sure, I would have liked to do the pomp-and-circumstance thing—but our team had a shot at the College World Series. To get to the Series, I'd traded my cap and gown for a catcher's mask in a heartbeat.

At the regional tournament, we played against three other schools and won our first three games in double elimination play. All we had to do was win one game of a doubleheader and we'd be in the Series. Our opponent was Florida State, a team that had already lost once and was one game from elimination. We played the first game and scored a lot of runs, but in the end, we lost it, 11 to 8.

My family was there for the tournament. They had driven in two cars from our home in Wilmington, Delaware—my dad in one car, my mom and two sisters in the other. Throughout the three-day tournament, they cheered on our team. Now we were down to the last game of the tournament, which was a must-win for Wake Forest.

The game started, and both teams struggled through inning after inning. By the seventh inning, the score was 1 to 1. Top of the eighth, I came up to bat—and I knocked one over the left field fence. I was delirious with joy as I rounded the bases. We were up by one run—*my* home run!—and the College World Series was just two innings away.

Or so I thought. By the end of the ninth, the score was 2 to 2 and we went into extra innings. Bottom of the eleventh, same score—until a Florida State runner scored, ending our season and our shot at the Series.

I walked off the field inconsolable. I hardly said a word to my family, even though they had driven nine hours and more than 500 miles to cheer for me. I'm ashamed to admit it, but I was so absorbed in my own disappointment that I wasn't very civil.

As I took off my shin guards and chest protector, my dad came up and said, "Tough break, son."

"Yeah, tough," I said.

"You almost had 'em," he said. "It was so close."

"Yeah, close."

My mom and sisters, Carol and Ruthie, were over by the car. They waved to me. I nodded back, unsmiling.

"Well, I guess we'll be going," my dad said. "I'm dropping Carol off in Washington, then I'll head home. Your mother and Ruthie are taking the other car to Wilmington."

"Okay," I said. "See you there."

It started raining as my teammates and I boarded the bus for the ride back to campus.

The next morning, four of my teammates and I loaded a car and headed north. They planned to drop me off at my home and then continue on. My buddies and I took our time, even stopping to watch a triple-A game in Richmond, Virginia, where we spent the night.

We got a late start the next morning and arrived in Wilmington around five that evening. I was surprised to see a lot of cars and people around our house. We pulled into the driveway. As I got out, my mother rushed up to me. Her eyes were red.

"Oh, Pat," she said, "Your father was in an accident after he left Carol in Washington."

I felt like I'd been punched in the solar plexus. "An accident?" I said. "How bad?"

"Pat, your father was killed."

My Second Father

While driving alone on the Washington/Baltimore Expressway in the wee hours of the morning, Dad apparently fell asleep at the wheel. His car veered into a bridge abutment, and he died instantly. No other cars were involved in the accident.

My father's death left a huge hole in my life. I often wished my last words to my dad had been more kind, more appreciative. My dad was my encourager and coach. He died right after I left college and just as I was entering the real world. I felt that I had lost the steady guiding hand I had always counted on. I had lost his advice, his experience, his love and his wisdom.

Two-and-a-half years after I lost my dad, I met Mr. R. E. Littlejohn. He became a second father to me. The influence of Mr. R. E. had such an impact on my life that when my first son was born in 1974, my wife and I named him James Littlejohn Williams—"James" after my birth father, Jim Williams, and "Littlejohn" after my second father, Mr. R. E.

It wasn't long after I started working for Mr. R. E.—actually, only a matter of days—before he spotted a glaring flaw in my temperament. He realized that I was a control freak. For a while, he allowed me to waste my time and energy in a futile effort to control every detail of the operation. Then he gave me some sage advice—which we'll get to in a moment.

Why was I such a fanatic about being in control? Only one reason: I was scared. Managing the Spartanburg Phillies was my first real job, and the season opened in just two months. I had a near-impossible challenge ahead of me, and I was scared to death of failure.

The baseball stadium at Duncan Park was run-down and dirty. The fields were overgrown with weeds. The paint on the fences was peeling. The restrooms were filthy beyond belief. When I first saw the place, I wondered how the two owners, Mr. R. E. and Leo Hughes, had let the place become so dilapidated. Then it hit me: These men had their own businesses to run. The reason they hired me to run the team was that they didn't have time to do it themselves. Fixing up the ballpark was *my* job.

So I took on the challenge of renovating that ballpark.
I worked 18 hours a day, 7 days a week. I had no social life
whatsoever. My waking hours were a blur of mowing grass,
painting outfield walls, building a new press box, refurbish-
ing locker rooms and remodeling restrooms. The ladies room
was my masterpiece. I put in air-conditioning, wallpaper, cur-
tains, full-length mirrors and a lush red carpet. To top it off,
I piped in soothing music, hired an attendant and had an
arrangement of fresh flowers brought in for every game.

I obsessed over every aspect of the ballpark. I carried a
huge key ring on my belt that gave me access to every area of
my universe—keys to the ballpark, the storage rooms, the
office and the restrooms, plus all my personal keys. I handled
all the selling, publicity and game-night promotions on my
own. After every game, I personally took the gate receipts to
the night deposit at the bank. I even set out the brooms so
that the park custodians would be ready to go the next
morning. I didn't trust anyone else to do these jobs because
I had to be in control. If I didn't do it myself, I was afraid it
wouldn't get done right.

By opening day, that once-dilapidated ballpark was a
showplace—the Taj Mahal of minor league baseball stadi-
ums. As opening day neared, Mr. R. E. kept in daily contact
with me. He often told me that he believed in me and that
he knew we were going to have a great season—pep talks
that really kept me motivated in the midst of the fears and
challenges I was facing. He praised everything I did right
and shrugged off my mistakes (which were many). I think he
figured that I would learn from my mistakes without having
them pointed out to me.

Mr. Littlejohn was my cheering section, and I could tell he wanted me to succeed and grow. I quickly grew to love him like a father.

The Ulcer King of Spartanburg

When you're running a minor league baseball team, you constantly confront two issues that largely determine the success or failure of your ball club:

1. *What kind of team will I have?* Even though I was the general manager, I had no control over the team. All the players were scouted, drafted and assigned by the major league front office. The executives in Philadelphia did whatever they wanted, and as a minor league operator, I had no say. Even though I had no control over the kind of team I had to work with, I agonized as if I did. I tormented myself (and my coaching staff) over such matters as batting order, pitching rotation and who was (or wasn't) playing well. Not surprisingly, all my pacing and fretting didn't change a thing.

2. *What kind of weather will I have on home games?* Obviously, I had no control over the weather—but did that stop me from worrying? No way! I lived with the constant fear that a few frog-strangling rainouts on game nights might ruin my entire season. I'd turn into an emotional

basket case whenever dark clouds loomed during the afternoon—and if those clouds ever
unleashed a downpour, I was a wreck!

I was the Ulcer King of Spartanburg. I paced, fretted
and fumed, wracking my brain for ways to assert my control
over those two uncontrollable issues. Mr. Littlejohn saw
what I was going through as a 24-year-old front-office neo-
phyte. He could tell that I was wearing out my stomach lining, fretting and worrying over the team and the weather.
He encouraged me from time to time to relax, take it easy
and try not to worry—but I couldn't help myself.

Finally, around the middle of our first season, Mr.
Littlejohn said, "Pat, come into my office. We need to have a
talk." As it turned out, it was Mr. Littlejohn who had to talk.
I had to listen.

"Pat," he said in that wonderful, deep, South Carolina
drawl of his, "how much control do you really think you have
with the Philadelphia office about the players we're getting?"

"None," I said.

"And just how much control do you think you have over
the weather?"

I had to admit that I didn't have any influence there
either.

"Well, Pat," he continued, "tell me this: How much control do you have over how much ice is in the drinks and how
hot the hot dogs are and how clean the ladies restroom is
and how creative your promotions are and how friendly and
personable your game night staff is? How much control do
you have over all those issues?"

I grinned sheepishly. "I see where you're going, Mr. R. E. You're right. I don't have a lot of control over any one of those issues."

"Well, Pat, why don't you focus on controlling the things that you can control and quit worrying about the team and the weather? It will make life so much simpler for you—and you won't have to swallow antacids by the handful anymore."

Four decades have come and gone since Mr. R. E. and I had that talk. In all the years since, I have recalled his advice literally thousands of times. I have applied his wise advice to both my professional career and my personal life: *Control what you can, and let go of everything else.*

I don't claim to have this principle perfected in my life—but I'm better at it than I used to be. I still worry about the things I can't control, but I don't obsess over them. I think about that principle every day, and whenever I'm tempted to try to control the uncontrollable and manage the unmanageable, I hear Mr. Littlejohn's voice in my mind: "Pat, just control what you can control, and let go of everything else."

Life has been so much simpler since he gave me that advice.

Giving Up on Solving the World's Problems

After many years as a general manager in the NBA, I called a press conference in Orlando and made this announcement: "Ladies and gentlemen of the press, I am hereby resigning as general manager of the universe. Over the years, I have tried to solve the world's problems, yet I have to admit that all of my efforts have had very little impact on global warming, the ozone layer, overpopulation, the national debt, the global economy and the crisis in the Middle East. As a result, I've decided to concentrate on controlling only those things that I have control over."

A reporter from *USA Today* stood up and said, "Mr. Williams, I understand that you have 19 children. Are you resigning as general manager of the universe in order to concentrate on controlling your kids?"

I laughed. "Are you kidding? My kids have all the answers. By the time the youngest turned 13, I had lost all control over them."

A correspondent from CNN stood up and asked, "Mr. Williams, if you've given up trying to solve the world's problems, and you've given up trying to control your kids, what *can* you control?"

"One thing," I replied. "I can control my attitude. No matter how bad things get, I can always choose my outlook on life. Every day, I get to pick my attitude for the day. And if I get to pick my attitude, I might as well pick a good one."

All right, I know what you're thinking. That press conference didn't really happen. Well, you're right, it didn't *literally* take place—but the fact is, I truly have made that decision in my own life. I have decided to control what I can control and let go of the rest.

Sure, I still care about the environment and social ills and peace and justice, and I do my part in all of those areas to make the world a better place. I still care about the choices my kids make, even when they don't always listen to me. I do what I can to help them make good choices.

But I'm not in control. I'm not the general manager of the universe. I'm not the general manager of my kids' lives. I've found that it's a full-time job just being the general manager of Pat Williams. If I can control my attitude and my behavior each day, it will be enough.

Don't Freak!

The term "control freak" is clearly not a compliment. A control freak is a person who has an excessive, obsessive, compulsive need to control people and situations.

It's normal to want to be in control of our lives and careers. It's unhealthy, however, to be so obsessed with control that we harm our relationships, make other people miserable and feel anxious and tense when we can't control every aspect of a situation. We need to be able to tolerate uncertainty and even a degree of chaos in our life.

Did you ever have a control freak for a boss? Remember how he or she made you feel? Controlling bosses delegate responsibility but no authority. They don't trust you, and they won't let you exercise any initiative or creativity. They're always looking over your shoulder and driving you crazy with their obsessive behavior. They make you hate your job.

One reason that control freaks are so unbearable is that they are totally self-centered. Because they demand to be in control, they care only about *their* needs and wants. *Your* feelings are of no interest to them. Make a decision and they'll reverse it—and probably humiliate you in front of your coworkers. Organizations headed by control freaks usually have high turnover and low morale.

Trying to coexist with a control freak is miserable enough. *Being* a control freak is even worse.

You may remember Judith Viorst as the author of the classic children's book *Alexander and the Terrible, Horrible, No Good, Very Bad Day*. She has also written a book for adults who are control freaks or who have to live around control freaks. After the release of her book *Imperfect Control: Our Lifelong Struggles with Power and Surrender*, she told an interviewer that a lot of people have a controlling streak in them.

"But," she added, "a full-fledged control freak is someone who can't stop controlling, controls inappropriately and controls all the time. They're really scared, and if they don't control every piece of a situation the world will turn to dust, the project will fail, their life will be ruined. And some of them are very anxious about being controlled, so it's a preemptive strike. If I don't control you, you'll control me."[1]

If you want to be cured of being a control freak, I have two words for you: *professional sports*. In the sports business, you soon discover that there are some factors you can control pretty well—and there are some factors you can't control worth beans. If you can't tell one from the other, you'll end up going crazy.

In sports, you can control your roster of players, your coaching staff and the training and physical conditioning of your team. You can control the execution of your game plan. You can coach your players to control the ball and control the clock.

But you can't control the surprises your opponent springs at you on the field or the court. You can't control what the referees and umpires think they see. You can't control serious injuries to key players. You can't control the outrageous things the reporters write about you on the sports page. You can't control the stuff the fans throw at you from the stands.

Legendary UCLA basketball coach John Wooden had a lot to say about what you can control, what you can't control and how to tell the difference. He once said, "Focus all your efforts on what is within your power to control. Physical conditioning is one of those things. How your mind functions is another." He recalled that he learned this lesson from his father. "My dad used to say, 'If you get caught up in things over which you have no control, it will adversely affect those things over which you have control.' You have little control over what criticism or praise outsiders send your way. Take it all with a grain of salt."

So when it comes to control, don't freak! Control what you can, and let go of everything else.

The Random Factor

Dennis Green, former head coach of the Minnesota Vikings, once observed, "Football is a strange game. It's played with a funny-shaped ball that bounces a lot of ways. As a head coach, you only work on the things you can control. You cannot control the bounce of the ball." Longtime Rams linebacker Jim Collins agreed. "You can't control the outcomes. Luck is and always will be a factor."

Now, I don't believe in "luck" in the sense of a capricious supernatural force that controls my destiny. But I do believe in the "random factor." In life, there are always variables you can't account for, factors you can't control. So, as Mr. R. E. taught me, you control what you can—but you have to let go of the random factors, the unexpected bounces that the ball of life sometimes takes.

Mickey Rivers was a major league baseball player in the 1970s and 1980s (he played with the Angels, Yankees and Rangers). Mickey was known for his speed and hitting—and for his quirky, but realistic, outlook on life. He once said, "There ain't no sense worryin' about things you got control over, 'cause if you got control over 'em, ain't no sense in worrying. And there ain't no sense worryin' about things you got no control over, 'cause if you got no control over 'em, ain't no sense worryin'."

Most of what happens to us—perhaps as much as 90 percent—is beyond our control. I can control the car I'm driving, but if the driver of the car behind me is text-messaging instead of watching the road, there's not a thing I can do to keep from being rear-ended. You may be diligent and hardworking in your job—but an industry-wide recession could cost you your job, and there's not a thing you can do about it.

Our lives are affected by the weather, politics, the economy, crime, family members, friends, and all sorts of random factors. When things happen that we can't control, we are forced to respond. Some people respond by ranting about the unfairness of life. Others respond by asking, "How can I turn this situation to my advantage? How can I learn a lesson from it? How can I redeem some benefit from it? At the very least, how can I find some detour around it so that I can keep moving toward my goals?"

Lou Holtz, the longtime head football coach at Notre Dame, is a big advocate of the Serenity Prayer, which was written in the 1930s by the American theologian Reinhold Niebuhr. It states:

> *God grant me the serenity to*
> *accept the things I cannot change,*
> *the courage to change the*
> *things I can, and the wisdom*
> *to know the difference.*

"Like a lot of people," says Holtz, "I've struggled with the things I cannot control. It was difficult to remain serene when the actions or inactions of others led to outcomes I thought were wrong. It's natural to become frustrated when things affect you that are beyond your control. That's why praying for serenity is so important in coaching."

As Jesus said, "Who of you by worrying can add a single hour to his life?" (Matt. 6:27). If we can stay focused on controlling the things we can control while letting go of the things we can't, then we will save ourselves a lot of time, worry and stomach lining.

The People Factor

In addition to the "random factor," there is the "people factor." People are just as uncontrollable as any blind force of nature. In fact, we're actually better off if we *don't try* to control other people. This is especially true in the business world.

You can never be successful in business by controlling the people who work with you or for you. Whether you are a boss, a mid-level manager or an employee, your goal should always be to empower, not control, the people around you. In *The People Principle,* Ron Willingham, speaker, author and founder of Integrity Systems, observes:

> Empowering people means, in a sense, relinquishing control. And many managers equate having control with how valuable they are to their organizations.
>
> This is bad thinking.
>
> Often, keeping control limits productivity. If you're a person who micromanages, you'll just naturally limit your productivity. There aren't enough hours in the day for you to be involved in every decision your people have to make. . . .
>
> Control is a paradoxical, illusional thing. Often when you think you have it, you don't. Often when you think having it is important to keep your job, you lose your position by hanging on to it. Control may give people a sense of power, but the more they rely on it, the more their chances of losing power increase.[2]

Success occurs when an enterprise grows beyond one person's ability to assert control. When the founder can no longer control every aspect of the organization, it means that people are empowered to make decisions and initiate actions that can produce great rewards.

Joe Born is an entrepreneur and founder of Neuros Technology, a Chicago-based manufacturer of audio and video devices. "Broadly speaking," he says, "entrepreneurs have to learn to give up control. It's painful. It's something I and every entrepreneur struggle with every day. I walk the halls of this company now, and there are meetings going on and I don't even know what they're about. It's very uncomfortable, when I used to know everything."

Herb Kelleher, cofounder and former CEO of Southwest Airlines, puts it more succinctly: "Never had control. Don't want control." John A. Byrne, senior writer at *Business Week*, agrees: "Companies that thrive will be led by people who understand that, in business as in nature, no one person can ever really be in control."

What is true in the business world is true in other organizations, including churches. Rick Warren, founding pastor of Southern California's Saddleback Church, said, "In any organization you have to decide whether you want growth or control. You cannot have both."

Even if you wanted to be able to control people, it's *impossible*. People are, by the very nature of human free will, uncontrollable. People will sometimes misunderstand you, misinterpret your actions, gossip about you, lie to you (or about you), criticize you, mistreat you or hate you—even when you've done nothing to deserve it. You cannot control them.

So what are you going to do? Are you going to marinate in anger and resentment over the people you can't control, or are you going to let go of such people, focus on the things you *can* control and get on with your life? It's totally up to you.

In his book *Goals*, self-help author Brian Tracy wrote, "Every time you criticize someone else, complain about something you don't like, or condemn someone else for something that they have done or not done, you trigger feelings of negativity and anger within yourself. And you are the one who suffers. Your negativity doesn't affect the other person at all. Being angry with someone is allowing him or her to control your emotions, and often the entire quality of your life, at long distance."[3]

It's true. If you do not control your emotions, you allow other people to control you. Booker T. Washington, author of *Up from Slavery*, put it this way: "I will let no man control me by making me hate him."

You can't control other people—and you shouldn't want to. It has been said that the only thing worse than a person you can't control is a person you can. So let go of the need to control other people and their behavior. Accept the fact that others will sometimes disappoint you and even turn against you. Be tolerant and forgiving. Take it in stride. You can't control what people do, but you can always control your attitude and your response.

Your Locus of Control

Psychologists tell us that people who feel that they are in control of their own lives tend to be happy, well-adjusted and successful. People who feel that their lives are controlled by outside forces see themselves as unhappy victims of fate. In psychology, this concept is known as "locus of control theory." This principle divides people into two groups: internals (those who see their lives as being under their own control) and externals (those who see their lives as being controlled by other people and outside forces and events).

The word "locus" means place, center or focus. If you feel that the place of control in your life is centered within you, then you feel confident, empowered and ready to take on the world. If you feel that the locus of control over your life is outside of you, that it's in the hands of other people or the hands of an uncaring fate, then you will feel powerless, fearful, resentful and depressed.

A student with a strong internal locus of control will say, when receiving a poor grade, "I earned this grade through my lack of effort." A student with an external locus of control will say, "I got this grade because my teacher hates me." If you have an external locus of control, you will fall into the habit of blaming other people for your problems while making excuses for yourself. You'll feel bitter, helpless and frustrated—and you'll see yourself as a failure in life. But if you have an internal locus of control, you'll face life with a confident can-do attitude that will enable you to excel and succeed.

People with an external locus of control see themselves as victims. People with an internal locus of control see themselves as victorious. Where is your locus of control? Do you feel controlled by family members, past events, an unhappy childhood, a miserable job, financial pressure or some other external force? If so, you need to change the way you look at your life. You need to acknowledge the simple but life-transforming fact that *you control you.*

Obviously, there are forces in your life that are beyond your control. If an earthquake or hurricane knocks down your house, there's not much you can do about that. But even when disaster strikes out of the blue, you can exercise internal control. You can choose your own attitude. You can choose how you will respond when things happen that you can't control. As someone once said, "If you want to be successful, put your effort into controlling the sail, not the wind."

Seven Aspects of Control

Once you acknowledge the fact that *you control you*, it's clear that you can control many more aspects of your life than you realize. Let me give you seven examples.

1. You Can Control Your Effort

Retired after 36 years as head basketball coach at the University of North Carolina at Chapel Hill, Dean Smith is a coaching legend. As a coach, he always insisted on his players controlling their level of effort. In his book *Carolina Way: Leadership Lessons from a Life in Coaching*, Coach Smith reflects:

> Maybe a player wasn't the fastest, the tallest, or the most athletic person on the court. In the course of any given game, that was out of his control. But each player could control the effort with which he played. "Never let anyone play harder than you," I told them. "That is part of the game you can control." If another team played harder than we did, we had no excuse for it. None.
>
> We worked on it in every practice. If a player didn't give maximum effort, we dealt with it right then. We stopped practice and had the entire team run sprints because of the offending player. We played a style of

basketball that was physically exhausting and made it impossible for a player to go full throttle for forty minutes. When he got tired, he flashed the tired signal (a raised fist) and we substituted for him. He could put himself back in the game once rested.

We didn't want tired players on the court, because they usually tried to rest on defense. That wouldn't work in our plan. Therefore, we watched closely in practice and in games to make sure players played hard. If they slacked up, it was important to catch them and get them out of the game, or if it occurred in practice, to have the entire team run.[4]

Tennis star James Blake started playing the game when he was 5 years old. At age 13, he was diagnosed with severe scoliosis, a deformative curvature of the spine. He wore a full back brace during every waking hour except when he was playing tennis. Inspired by his hero, Arthur Ashe, Blake pursued his dream. Named Rookie of the Year in 2001, Blake seemed destined for greatness. Then, in 2004, while practicing for the Masters, Blake ran into a net post and severely injured his neck. He developed facial paralysis and blurred vision. He thought he was finished in tennis.

At that same time, Blake's father, Tom, was dying of stomach cancer. Before he passed away, Blake's dad gave him this advice: "You can't control your level of talent, but you can control your level of effort." James Blake remembered that advice. After recovering from his injuries, he played with a newfound intensity and became an even more dominant force in the game. He's living proof of his father's sound advice. No matter what happens in your life, you can always control your effort.

2. You Can Control Your Time

If you want to control your life, you must control your time. Your life is made up of a finite number of heartbeats, seconds and hours, which add up to a finite number of years. People speak so casually about "killing time," but those who kill time are actually killing themselves, moment by precious moment. If life is infinitely precious, then so is time. We don't have a moment to waste.

Every morning, at the stroke of midnight, you receive an incalculable gift—the gift of 86,400 seconds. For the next 24 hours, you can spend those 86,400 seconds any way you choose. Working toward your goals. Sleeping. Reading a book. Thinking. Writing your novel. Taking a night class. Working out at the gym. Serving food at a homeless shelter. Tutoring a child. Hanging out with friends. Playing video games. Twiddling your thumbs. Watching the idiot box. It's your choice—and come midnight, your day's allotment of 86,400 seconds is all used up.

How did you spend your time? Did you invest it or squander it? It's your life. The locus of control is within you. Nobody gets any more time in a day than anyone else. Everyone gets the same 86,400-second allotment. If you fail to manage your own finite allotment of time, you have no one to blame but you.

People who control their time well are a valuable human resource. They are the hard-charging entrepreneurs, the prolific writers and artists, the reliable employees, the hardworking craftspeople and tradespeople, the dedicated health-care professionals and the diligent researchers and scientists that society counts on to get the job done. Employers know the value of people who respect the precious value of a fleeting moment of time—and they invariably single out such people for reward and promotion.

If you want to control your life and control your success, then you must control your time. Begin now with the 86,400 seconds that are yours today. Control each moment, wring every possible advantage and benefit from each passing second, and you will control your life.

3. You Can Control Your Impulses

The ability to control our impulses is what is commonly called "self-control." Self-control means saying no to instant gratification in order to say yes to delayed satisfaction. It means that we know what is truly important in life, and we practice the self-discipline to achieve it. It means that we set worthwhile goals in life and make the daily, moment-by-moment decisions that keep us moving toward those goals.

A person with self-control says, "I can resist my impulse to have an ice cream sundae. I choose to have a protein shake and spend an hour at the gym instead. Having a fit and healthy body is more important to me than a guilty, calorie-laden pleasure." A person with self-control says, "My marriage and my integrity mean more to me than a casual hook-up for sex. I choose to say no to my impulses in order to keep what is truly important to me—the love of my life and my self-respect." A person with self-control says, "I refuse to squander my money on a lot of junk that will mean nothing to me next week. I refuse to go into debt so that I can eat out every night or drink Starbucks five times a day. I choose to resist my spending impulses in order to build wealth and save for the things that truly matter."

We all have impulses that if yielded to will build self-destructive habits into our lives—impulses to lie, cheat, steal, overeat, overspend, overindulge in alcohol, take drugs, gamble and yield to lust and sexual immorality. If we want to live healthy, happy and successful lives, we must master our impulses.

On the ABC newsmagazine *20/20*, reporter John Stossel reported that self-control is one of the most important indicators of future success. He interviewed the noted social psychologist Dr. Roy F. Baumeister, who is currently a professor of psychology at Florida State University in Tallahassee. Dr. Baumeister said, "If you look at the social and personal problems facing people in the United States—we're talking drug and alcohol abuse, teen pregnancy, unsafe sex, school failure, shopping problems, and gambling—over and over, the majority of them have self-control failure as central to them. Studies show that self-control does predict success in life over a very long time."

Note that last statement: "*Self-control does predict success in life.*" Put another way: People who show self-control tend to lead successful lives. People who don't, don't.

In the *20/20* report, Stossel showed video of an experiment conducted at a nursery school. "By testing how well four-year-olds can resist temptation," he explained, "researchers say they can predict what kind of adults they're likely to be. In the experiment, the kids are given a choice: They'll get five pieces of candy if they can wait ten minutes until the teacher comes back into the room—or just two pieces if they can't wait and give in to the temptation before the ten minutes is up.

"So the kids tried. It wasn't easy. Most fidgeted and looked as if they were being tortured. Some touched the candy. One boy counted the candy—maybe to remind himself that five is more than two. One girl looked heavenward as she waited, seeming to ask for God's help. Seven of the nine kids we tested lasted the full ten minutes."

Stossel talked to a four-year-old girl named Heather. "Did you put your hand over the bell and think about ringing it?" he asked.

"Yeah," the girl said, "but I didn't ring the bell."

"Why not?" asked Stossel.

"Because the teacher said I could have five candies if I waited."

"And you got five?"

"Uh-huh."

"Was it worth waiting for?"

"It was hard."

Researchers at Columbia University had actually conducted a similar (but more in-depth) study about three decades earlier. The Columbia study tested a large number of children to see which ones would demonstrate self-control and which ones would not. The rules were the same: Kids could have two candies now or resist temptation and get five candies later.

The children were followed up at intervals over the next 30 years. The results were striking and unmistakably clear:

The children who demonstrated self-control in the experiment clearly were more successful in life than those who did not. They had high SAT scores, fewer problems with the law and, for girls, fewer teen pregnancies. Dr. Baumeister concluded that if we want to be happy, healthy, successful human beings, "forget about self-esteem; concentrate on self-control."[5]

4. You Can Control Your Attitude

"The greatest revelation of our generation," said pioneering psychologist William James, "is the discovery that human beings, by changing the inner attitudes of their minds, can change the outer aspects of their lives." We tend to think our happiness is determined by our circumstances: "If I just had enough money" or "If I had a better job" or "If I'd gotten better breaks in life—then I'd be happy." This is faulty thinking. Happiness is not the result of our circumstances but of the attitude we have toward our circumstances.

Hugh Downs, former host of ABC's *20/20* and NBC's *Today Show*, said, "A happy person is not a person in a certain set of circumstances, but rather a person with a certain set of attitudes." And the late, great golf legend Payne Stewart once said, "A bad attitude is a bigger handicap than a bad swing."

Scott Hamilton, the Olympic gold medal-winning figure skater (Sarajevo, 1984) is famed not only for his performances but also for his buoyant personality in the face of personal adversity. As a child, he suffered from a mysterious illness that was never diagnosed, but which inhibited his growth. As a skater, however, Scott turned his slight 5' 2" 108-pound frame into an advantage on the ice. In 1997, he underwent a life-and-death struggle with cancer; and in 2004, he was treated for a benign brain tumor. When people commiserated with him about his problems, he replied, "Adversity is not a handicap. The only handicap in life is a bad attitude."

Controlling your attitude is the key to overcoming the worst circumstances in life. In *The Winner's Edge*, Denis Waitley tells about Air Force Colonel George Hall, a pilot who was shot down over North Vietnam. He was captured and spent more than five years in solitary confinement as a prisoner of war.

Hall survived the years of alternating terror and boredom by mentally leaving his prison and imagining himself at the Pebble Beach golf course on the California coast. He imagined every detail—the fragrance of fresh-cut grass, the cool salt breeze from the Pacific, the grip of the club in his hands, the satisfying rattle of the ball in the cup. In his mind, he played each fairway, putted each green and downed a celebratory drink at the Tap Room, the historic nineteenth hole at Pebble Beach.

Every day for more than five years, Colonel Hall played a perfect game of golf in his imagination. Why? Because he knew that he could either resign himself to hopelessness or he could set his mind free to play golf on the cypress-lined coast of northern California.

When Colonel Hall was released from prison and returned to the States, one of the first things he did was go to Pebble Beach and play a game of golf—this time with real clubs and a real ball. His first time out on the links, he shot an eye-popping 76! This was an absolutely phenomenal achievement for a man who had spent more than five years in a tiny concrete cell in the Hanoi Hilton. Asked how he did it, he replied, "In the past five-and-a-half years, I never putted a green in more than two strokes."

That is the power of the human attitude under control. Psychiatrist and Holocaust survivor Viktor Frankl put it this way: "The last of the human freedoms is the freedom to choose one's attitude in any given set of circumstances."

5. You Can Control Your Anger

Someone once asked John Wooden, "As a coach, did you ever lose your temper?" He replied, "I always told my players to control their tempers, and I couldn't very well expect them to if I wasn't setting a good example myself. I lost my temper once in a while. But I never lost control."

Many people don't know that they *can* control their anger. Some have never even tried. It's normal to feel angry from time to time. But we can control how we respond to feelings of anger. Some people think that "venting" anger is a healthy way to get the anger out of your system. Actually, "venting"—giving way to anger by blowing up, shouting, pounding tables or throwing lamps—only makes the situation worse. Angry actions trigger strong physiological responses, including the release of stress hormones. Our ability to think rationally is diminished. And when we vent, we look foolish.

When you feel angry, verbalize—don't vent. State your feelings as calmly as possible and in a way that respects the feelings of others. Direct your anger at problems, not people. When you talk through your anger instead of putting your fist through a wall, you show that you are in control of you. And when you control you, you control the situation.

6. You Can Control Your Fear

Another key to success is the ability to control our fear. People who control their fear are empowered to act boldly, confidently and courageously. What is courage? It's not the absence of fear. It's the ability to *control* our fear so that our fear won't control us.

Even heroes experience fear. They simply respond to their fear in a different way than cowards do. As John Wayne once put it, "Courage is being scared to death but saddling up anyway."

Courage is also closely connected with faith. If we truly trust God to be in control of our life, then what do we have to fear? As God told Moses and the people of Israel, "Be strong and courageous. Do not be afraid or terrified . . . for the LORD your God goes with you; he will never leave you nor forsake you" (Deut. 31:6).

7. You Can Control Your Responses

You can control your response to crises, problems, disappointments, obstacles and opposition. When you demonstrate that you are cool, calm and controlled under fire, you show that you are ready for greater responsibility and promotion. Civil War general Robert E. Lee said, "I cannot trust a man to control others who cannot control himself."

One of my all-time sports heroes is Mike Schmidt, probably the greatest third baseman in baseball history (my son Michael is named after him). When he played for the Philadelphia Phillies, he was known as "Captain Cool" for his calm self-control under pressure. Mike Schmidt once talked about the qualities he admired in a baseball manager. The number-one trait he listed was the ability to maintain control in a crisis.

"A manager has numerous opportunities to blow his stack in your typical ballgame," he said. "Being able to remain calm and positive in the teeth of adversity is an absolute necessity. Everyone in the dugout checks out the manager's reaction when things go sour. Any display of excessive anger, disgust or disappointment adds to the burden of the player's failure. Whatever he's feeling inside, a manager must convey to his players a sense that all is well, that somebody will get a key hit or make the right pitch next time."

You Control *You*

When I was general manager of the Atlanta Hawks, I attended the Braves-Dodgers home opener, a night game on April 8, 1974. Why do I remember that game so distinctly? Because a record was on the line. The immortal Henry Louis Aaron was at the plate, and he had already tied Babe Ruth's record of 714 career home runs. Aaron was aiming to break it.

That year, as Hank Aaron made his run at the record, he received an incredible volume of mail—more than 930,000 letters in all. Around 100,000 of those letters were hate letters and death threats. Put yourself in Hank Aaron's place: How secure would you feel walking onto the field surrounded by thousands of people, any one of whom might be a nut case with a weapon and a crazy grudge?

I will never forget the moment when that Dodgers pitcher Al Downing hurled the ball over the plate. Hank Aaron connected. The crack of his bat echoed across the sta-

dium—and that ball was gone. The fans went wild. Babe
Ruth's record was shattered like the sound barrier.

As Aaron rounded the bases, a couple of fans ran out onto
the field toward Aaron. Were they the ones who had threat-
ened him? No, they were cheering and celebrating—though,
for a moment, all those hate letters must have flashed through
Aaron's mind.

Hank Aaron's teammates ran onto the field and surrounded him, whooping and yelling. Amid all those big,
burly Atlanta ballplayers, I noticed one small, elderly African-
American woman. She reached out and grabbed hold of the
new home-run king, and she refused to let go.

Aaron turned, saw the woman and shouted, "Mom!
What are *you* doing out here?"

"Baby," Hank's mother replied, "if they're gonna get
you, they've gotta get me first!"

We have to admire a man who, in spite of 100,000 hate
letters and death threats, steps calmly onto the field and,
with total control, knocks the ball right into the record
books. Where does a man learn that kind of control in the
face of threat and opposition? Well, he probably learned a
lot of it from his mom, because she was at his side when the
chips were down.

You can't control all the circumstances life throws at
you. And you can't control all the random factors that come
at you in sports, business or life. You can't control the past
and you can't predict the future; but you can seize this present moment—and you can control *you*.

There is always an internal locus of control that you can
tap into so that you can control your effort, time, impulses,

attitude, anger, fear and responses to life's problems and challenges.

If you control *you*, then you're well on your way to a successful life.

Chapter 2

Be Patient

My first season as general manager of the Spartanburg Phillies ended in late August 1965. I had turned 25 in May, and we had enjoyed a good year. True, we didn't have a very good team on the field. The Phillies organization in Philadelphia had tried to get us some talented players, but the fact is, our ball club was not very competitive.

But boy did we promote baseball in Spartanburg! In a town with a population of 50,000, we drew 114,000 people to 60 home games (up from 30,000 the previous season). I was named Executive of the Year in the Western Carolinas League and got some good national publicity. So I was off to a great start after just one year as a minor league general manager.

There was just one problem: It all went to my head.

I remember the night after our last home game, after the crowds had left and Duncan Park was quiet. It was a warm, humid night, and Mr. R. E. and I walked out to the parking lot and got in his car. He was going to give me a ride home—but he didn't turn the key. We just sat there with the windows rolled down, basking in the glow of the Duncan Park stadium lights, talking about the year we'd had.

For six intense months, from mid-February to the end of August, I had poured everything I had into that season, and we had done well. Mr. Littlejohn began talking about our next season, and the season beyond that. "This is just the beginning, Pat," he said with a satisfied smile. "You're off to a great start. You got the stadium whipped into shape. Your promotions have expanded the fan base. The whole county is talking about the Spartanburg Phillies. Wait and see, Pat. Next season will be even bigger and better."

"Next season?" I said. "Mr. R. E., I don't think I'll be here next season."

His smile faded. "Pat, after a season like this one, you're certainly not thinking of quitting, are you? Your job isn't done yet."

"I've left the place in good shape for the next guy," I said. "I've already proved myself in the minor leagues. I'm ready for the big leagues."

Mister R. E. sighed. "Pat," he said, "you think you're ready to move on because you've got one good year under your belt. I'm telling you it could have been an even better year. The real measure of success is how well you can build on what you've begun. You're 25 years old. You've got time. Be patient, Pat. Be patient."

"But you said it yourself: We had a great season! Within a few days, I'll get a call from the Yankees, the Dodgers, the Cubs—or maybe even my beloved Phillies! I appreciate everything you've done for me, Mr. R. E., but I'm ready to move up. And when that call comes, I've got to answer it."

Patience Pays Off

I must have looked like an absolute fool to Mr. Littlejohn. He knew I was living in a dream world. I'm so glad he didn't laugh at me, because that probably would have destroyed me. Instead, he just quietly repeated his wise counsel. "Be patient, Pat. Be patient."

Patient? Me? I ask you: Is there anything more impatient and impetuous than a young career-minded guy in his twenties? The way I saw it, nobody ever got anywhere by being patient. Success didn't come to those who were patient—it came to those who knew what they wanted and went out and got it. When Mr. Littlejohn counseled me to be patient, he might as well have been shouting from another planet, because I couldn't hear him.

Then he said something I didn't understand at the time, but which I've since learned is absolutely true. "Pat," he said, "you can go to the big leagues from Spartanburg—you can get there in one leap. You know how it is for a player. You move up from rookie to single-A to double-A to triple-A to the big leagues—and for baseball executives, it's usually the same progression. Pat, you can go straight to the big leagues from Spartanburg, but you've got to be patient. You can't prove yourself in one season. You've got to prove that you can do it season after season in the same location."

"But—"

"Hear me out, Pat. There are a lot of one-time salesmen out there. They can sell up a storm—once. They'll promise anything to make a sale, but nobody will buy from them a second time. My advice, Pat, is to come back and do it again next year. Prove this wasn't a fluke. Prove that you can do great things again and again."

Well, I was sure that Mr. R. E. didn't know what he was talking about. He had his old-fashioned ideas and his old-fashioned values, and they just didn't fit with my hard-charging ambition and my impatience. Soon that phone would ring and I would be called up to the big leagues. Then Mr. R. E. would see that I was right.

But the Yankees didn't call that week. And I didn't hear from the Dodgers, the Cubs or my beloved Phillies either. Soon, I was forced to the conclusion that maybe, just maybe, Mr. R. E. was right.

I came back for the second year—and what a season that was! Just as Mr. R. E. had predicted, we had an even better year—and we even had a great team. The Spartanburg Phillies finished the season with a 91-35, .722 record (including a 25-game winning streak), a league-leading .275 batting average and a circuit-best 715 runs. We generated a lot of excitement that year with a double-play combination that would go on to star for the Philadelphia Phillies, second baseman Denny Doyle and shortstop Larry Bowa.

So I learned that Mr. Littlejohn was right all along. Patience paid off.

The Most Impatient Person on God's Green Earth

In July 1968, during my fourth season in Spartanburg, I walked into my office and saw a phone message slip on my desk. It said that I had received a call from Jack Ramsay, and I was to call him back at a number in Inglewood, California.

I thought, *Whoa! What's this about?* The only Jack Ramsay I knew was the one who had coached basketball so successfully at St. Joseph's College in Philadelphia, before becoming general manager of the NBA's Philadelphia 76ers. It couldn't be *that* Jack Ramsay—he didn't even know me. I returned the call and sure enough, it *was* that Jack Ramsay.

"Have you been following what's been happening with our team?" he asked.

He was referring to one of the biggest trade deals in the history of professional sports. Yes, I certainly had been following it!

"Well, I'm out here in L. A.," he said, "to work out the final details of our trade with the Lakers. We'll be getting Darrall Imhoff, Archie Clark and Jerry Chambers in exchange for Wilt Chamberlain. The trade will be announced later this afternoon. I'm going to coach the team this season, and that won't leave me much time to manage the front office. We need a business manager, and I've been hearing good things about the job you're doing in Spartanburg. Would you like the job?"

"I sure would!"

"Fine, Pat," he said. "Come on up to Philadelphia in a few days. We'll hammer out the details."

As I flew up for the interview, my head was swimming. From the time I was in elementary school, I had been focused on a career in baseball. Suddenly, out of the blue, I had a chance to move to the National Basketball Association—which, as they say, was "a whole new ballgame."

I interviewed—and Jack Ramsay gave me the job. That was the beginning of a career in pro basketball that has spanned 40 years. Mr. Littlejohn had called it: "Pat," he told me, "be patient. You can go to the big leagues from Spartanburg."

So my question for you is: Where is your "Spartanburg"? Fact is, you're probably in your own Spartanburg right now. You're young and ambitious, you're eager to leave your mark on the world and, let's face it, *you're impatient* to do it.

Hey, there's no shame in that. I'm the most impatient person on God's green earth. My most natural inclination is to say, "Don't make me wait! I want it done now! Why isn't everybody jumping?"

Whenever I start feeling that way, whenever I start getting impatient with people or my circumstances, with my family or with God, I hear that voice speaking to me in that rich Carolina drawl: "Be patient, Pat. Be patient."

Old Advice for a New Era

Napoleon Hill (1883-1970) invented the personal success genre with his bestselling book *Think and Grow Rich*. He once said, "Patience, persistence, and perspiration make an unbeatable combination for success." Is that old-fashioned advice for a bygone era, or is patience still a virtue in this Internet-speed world?

I know that you have grown up in a point-and-click culture. You don't want to sit still and wait for life to begin. You are restless, busy, active and engaged. You go after what you want. Even at the office you're text messaging and video gaming while talking to clients on the phone and keeping one eye peeled for the boss. You're full of bravado and brio, and you just can't wait for the future to arrive—and I applaud that. I like your drive, my friend.

A few short decades ago, I *was* you. The advice to "be patient" didn't make any more sense to me then than it does to you now. But think about it.

Impatience drives bad decision-making. Impatience causes people to tromp the accelerator in order to beat the red light at the intersection or the crossing arms at the railroad tracks—and those impatient decisions sometimes result in tragedy and death. A lot of lives would be saved if drivers would patiently remind themselves that slowing down and waiting for a light to change could add decades to their life span.

It was an impatient decision that caused the space shuttle *Challenger* to explode 73 seconds into its tenth mission on January 28, 1986, killing seven crew members. Engineers at the Utah factory that built the shuttle's solid rocket boosters repeatedly warned NASA not to launch in extreme cold. The rubber O-rings that sealed the joints of the boosters became dangerously brittle and leaky in low temperatures. The temperature of the booster casing was measured at 8 degrees Fahrenheit that morning—well below the minimum temperature allowed for launch.

The engineers argued strenuously with NASA managers, trying to stop the launch. One NASA manager swore, and replied, "When do you want me to launch? Next April?" The space agency was impatient to maintain a vigorous launch schedule and prove that the shuttle was dependable.

When the engineers refused to agree in writing that the launch was safe, the NASA managers simply overruled them.

As the *Challenger* blasted off from the launch pad on that cold January morning, the engineers in Utah watched on television, silently praying. Seventy-three seconds later, their worst fears came true. When the shuttle exploded, they knew exactly what went wrong: NASA had made an impatient decision.

Impatience was also a major factor in the financial implosion of the Enron Corporation. One of the major players in the debacle was Enron's chief financial officer, Andrew Fastow, who skimmed $30 million from the company while shareholders lost more than $70 billion. Fastow was largely responsible for creating the complex network of limited partnerships the company used to conceal its debts and losses. Experts agree that Fastow's decision-making processes were driven by impatience.

In their book on the scandal, *Smartest Guys in the Room*, Bethany McLean and Peter Elkind wrote, "Not yet thirty years old, Fastow was already getting impatient" to score big promotions and pay raises at Enron.[1] And Associated Press writer Brad Foss wrote, "Former Enron employees who interacted with Fastow describe an executive intrigued by creative thinking yet impatient with those who didn't see things his way."[2] Financial writer Tom Fowler of the *Houston Chronicle* observed that "smart, bold and aggressive people" like Andrew Fastow "tend to get impatient with rules."[3]

One hasty, impatient decision could ruin your life. One moment of patient reflection could prevent disaster. Mr. Littlejohn's advice to me is as sound today as it was when I was a young man just starting out in life: "Be patient, Pat. Be patient."

Motivational speaker and author Wayne Dyer says, "Infinite patience brings immediate results." It's paradoxical but true. If you want to get places fast in this world, you have to be patient.

Many people, especially the young, mistake patience for passivity. They think that "Be patient" means "Be inactive." Authentic patience is truly a form of action. My friend Doc Rivers, who is currently head coach of the Boston Celtics, puts it this way: "I believe in pushy patience." Guy Kawasaki, one of the marketing geniuses behind the success of the Apple Macintosh (and who is currently a Silicon Valley venture capitalist), says, "Patience is the art of concealing your impatience."

The great thinkers of history have always regarded patience as a form of positive action, not passive inaction. John Wesley, the eighteenth-century English minister who cofounded the Methodist movement, said, "Though I am always in haste, I am never in a hurry." Inventor Thomas Edison said, "Everything comes to him who hustles while he waits." And former British prime minister Margaret Thatcher said, "I am extraordinarily patient, provided I get my own way in the end."

That's the kind of patience I'm talking about: pushy patience, focused patience, active patience—the kind of patience that moves us steadily and inexorably toward our goals. This kind of patience is the exact opposite of weakness or passivity or twiddling our thumbs. In fact, it is highly concentrated strength.

Wait for Your Pitch

Harvey Mackay, author of *Swim with the Sharks Without Being Eaten Alive*, related this story in sales and marketing management:

> The Japanese are masters of managing goals over time. When I visited Japan in 1983, we had a series of seminars in which we heard speeches from the leaders of Japan's largest industrial concerns, including Sony, Mitsubishi, and Matsushita Electric. When the 88-year-old president of Matsushita addressed us, he spoke eloquently and profoundly. But I was most impressed by this exchange:
>
> Question: "Mr. President, does your company have any long-range goals?"
>
> Answer: "Yes."
>
> Question: "How long are your long-range goals?"
> Answer: "Two hundred and fifty years."
> Question: "What do you need to carry them out?"
> Answer: "Patience."[4]

How does patience help you achieve your ambitious goals and dreams?

First, *patience is a leadership quality*. When you demonstrate patience as well as ambition, your bosses are able to see that you have what it takes to lead. Industrialist Henry Ford once said, "Patience and foresight are vital for success, and the man who lacks patience is not cut out for responsibilities in business." When your bosses see that you have that paradoxical spark of ambition combined with patience, you will get the rewards and promotion you deserve.

Second, *patience is a negotiating skill.* The late sports agent Mark McCormack put it this way: "Patience may be a virtue, but in negotiating, it is a weapon of incalculable power. If you can out-wait the other side, you can usually out-negotiate them."

Third, *patience is a character trait* and a personal discipline that gives you a competitive edge over your impatient peers and coworkers. Impatient people take ethical shortcuts that often destroy reputations and careers. Impatient people make unreasonable demands for advancement that actually side-track their careers.

Rick Pitino, head basketball coach at the University of Louisville, observes that many people "have no patience, no sense of paying their dues or waiting their turn. They want instant gratification, instant rewards and, if they don't get them from you, they will be looking for someone else to obtain them. Invariably they also don't have a lot of discipline either."

Fourth, *patience helps you respond more effectively* to the frustrations, annoyances and problems that are a part of everyday life. When an impatient person gets stuck in traffic, he becomes negative and angry, his blood pressure goes up and he loses his perspective on life. When a patient person gets stuck in traffic, even if it makes him late for an important appointment, he maintains his perspective. He remembers that in the grand scheme of things, being a little late is not such a big deal. It's hardly in the same category with a terrorist attack or a diagnosis of cancer. He makes a call and reschedules his meeting, he listens to music or a book on CD, he plans the rest of his day, he prays and meditates—he finds good ways to make use of his downtime.

Patience is the key to achieving our goals. The impatient person, when he plants a seed in the ground, continually digs up the dirt to see if the roots have started to grow. But a patient person puts the seed in the ground, waters the soil every day and waits for the plant to sprout, grow and bear fruit. The ancient Chinese had a proverb: "Patience is power. With time and patience, the mulberry leaf becomes silk." And the ancient Hebrews had a similar proverb: "Through patience a ruler can be persuaded, and a gentle tongue can break a bone" (Prov. 25:15).

It's normal to be impatient when you're young, but the sooner you learn patience, the more effective you'll be in life. Pastor and author Charles Swindoll observed, "It occurs to me that I've never met anyone young and patient. (To be honest, I've not met many old and patient folks, either.) We're all in a hurry. We don't like to miss one panel of a revolving door. Patience comes hard in a hurry-up society. Yet it's an essential quality, cultivated only in extended periods of waiting."

Coach John Wooden understands how different generations view patience. He wrote:

> Patience is the ability to wait and calmly persevere. We all grow impatient, but some people have more trouble waiting than others do. We tend to forget that all good things take time. . . . Youth can be impatient. Young people have a tendency to want to change more things more quickly. The mistake they

make is that they see all change as progress, and they fail to see the benefit of waiting.

In general, I think we tend to get more patient as we grow older. We don't ruffle as easily. Things don't seem to be as urgent. But older people tend to forget that there is no progress without change. Any organization that isn't moving forward is actually going backward. It is impossible to maintain the status quo; therefore, change is inevitable. The issue is how fast should it come?[5]

In chapter 1, I recalled the day when I saw Hank Aaron break Babe Ruth's home-run record. Aaron later talked about the secret of his success as a hitter. "I have to admit," he said, "that some pitchers worked me over pretty good with a certain pitch before I started getting even. The thing I had on my side was patience. Patience, which is really the art of waiting, is something you pick up pretty naturally when you grow up black in Alabama. When you wait all your life for respect and equality in a seat in the front of the bus, it's nothing to wait a little for a slider, inside."

Aaron particularly needed patience when he faced Johnny Podres, the great Dodgers pitcher. "Johnny Podres had a great change-up that gave me fits," Hank recalled. "One game, I made up my mind that I would wait as long as I had to until I got a change-up from him. The first time, he threw me a fastball, and I took it for a strike. Then he threw me two more and I took them for strikes. The same thing happened again the next time. He struck me out twice, and I never even swung the bat. The third time, I was still waiting for the change-up and, when he finally threw it, I hit it over the left-field fence. As I recall, it seems like it might have won the game."

Another great pitcher, Jim "Mudcat" Grant, vividly remembered the patience of Henry Aaron as the secret to his success: "Hank Aaron was the best hitter I have ever faced. Like Ted Williams, he had the patience to wait for his pitch and then he hit it hard."

So if you want to make your mark on the world—whether it's the world of sports, the business world or whatever your world may be—take a page from Hank Aaron's book. Wait for your pitch—then hit it out of the park.

Be patient.

Patience and Decision-Making

"Patience," said Saint Augustine, "is the companion of wisdom." Wise people keep their cool in a crisis. They take time to think and consider their situation and their options before they act. By their calm, patient example, they inspire confidence in the people around them.

Life is filed with deadlines and emergencies. When we are under pressure, we are easily tempted to panic and make an impulsive decision. We say, "I don't have time to think! I've got to act *now*!" But patience, planning and cool thinking are indispensable in a crisis. A noted surgeon once observed, "If I knew I only had five minutes to perform a delicate operation, I would spend the first two minutes planning the procedure." So when the pressure's on, take time to pray, to prioritize and to plan.

As baseball executive Branch Rickey put it, "You can't solve everything in a minute. Make time your ally. Delay sharp action." When seconds count, be patient—and *think*.

And when you think, take time to look at your problem from all angles. Often a seemingly insoluble crisis can be disassembled into bite-sized chunks. When you break big problems into a lot of little problems, you can more easily solve the big problems one step at a time.

When faced with a crisis, don't panic. Don't be stampeded by fear. Be patient. Golfer Jack Nicklaus said, "Impatience breeds hastiness, and the hastier you get, the less clearly and coolly you are able to think. These days, the way we live our personal and business lives tends to push us toward having less and less patience. If you are impatient, you cannot sustain greatness."

Impatient action almost always produces costly mistakes. Charles F. Knight, who guided the fortunes of Emerson Electric Co., once said, "Every mistake I made (and we all make mistakes) came because I didn't take the time to get the facts."

Self-help author Brian Tracy observed, "In a fast-paced, constantly changing world, an important habit . . . is the habit of thinking before acting. Often, when we are pressured from all sides with decisions that have to be made, we leap to conclusions and make decisions without carefully considering all the possible ramifications of those decisions. . . . Make it a habit of asking for a day, or a weekend, or even a week or a month, before you make a final decision. Put it off as long as possible. The very act of allowing the various pieces of information to settle in your brain will enable you to make a much better decision later on than you might have made if you decided too quickly. It's amazing how many people say, 'If I had just thought about that for a little while, I would have made a completely different decision.' This is almost always the case."

You won't always have the luxury of taking a week or a month to make a decision. Sometimes you only have a minute or two. If that's all you have, take that time to think carefully about your decision. Then, when it's time to act, take a deep breath and act boldly and confidently.

Let me suggest five principles for patient, wise decision-making, even in times of pressure and crisis:

1. *Seek wise counsel.* Gather as much information, insight and advice as you have time to gather. Poor decisions tend to be made in an information vacuum. The more you know, the better your decision-making ability.

2. *Take time to think and pray.* After gathering advice and opinions, sit down alone and sort through your options in a calm, unhurried setting. Apply reason to the situation. Pray about it. Listen for God's guidance. Ask yourself, *What would be the wise thing to do in this situation?*

3. *Stop thinking about the problem for a while.* Often, you are just too close to the situation to make a high-quality decision. So take a breather and take your mind off the situation for a while.

You may find that while jogging, walking the treadmill, taking a swim or just showering for five minutes, the perfect solution will pop into your mind seemingly out of nowhere. Clearing your conscious mind helps you receive insights via your brain's natural intuitive processes. Often, your pre-conscious mind will supply the key insight that your rational, logical mind has been missing.

4. *Default to no.* If, after following the previous three steps, you are still not sure which way to go, the best answer is usually no. It's easier to change a no decision to yes than to reverse a yes decision you've already made.

5. *Once you've decided, act firmly.* Don't hesitate or fret. Act decisively. Demonstrate courage and conviction—then do everything you can to successfully implement your choice. Odds are, you've made the right decision—and people will be amazed at how smart and decisive you are.

When you have a crucial decision to make, patience is the key to knowing *when* to act—and when *not* to act. In his book *Never Wrestle with a Pig*, Mark McCormack tells about watching game warden Ian Player at work in the largest game preserve in the Natal province in South Africa. Ian, the brother of South African golfer Gary Player (one of McCormack's clients), had to deal with poachers who were

rapidly killing off the population of endangered white rhi-
noceroses. To preserve the species, Ian had to round them
up and ship them to zoos around the world.

To capture the rhinos, Ian would lead a crew into the
bush. When they had spotted a rare white rhino, he would
shoot the animal with a tranquilizer dart and follow at a
respectful distance. Years of experience gave Ian the ability
to read a rhino's behavior. When the rhinoceros became
wobbly enough to capture, Player and his crew would back
the truck up to the animal.

Player needed patience in order to be successful. If he
moved the truck in too early, the rhino would not be suffi-
ciently tranquilized and would charge them. But if he moved
the truck in too late, the rhino would fall on its side and be
too heavy to load into the truck.

"With practice," McCormack wrote, "Ian became very
adept at this. He learned everything about the white rhino's
movements and quickly developed the perfect combination
of patience and decisive action that let him save the species.
That's the image I have of Ian Player: forever watching, forever patient, forever waiting for the decisive clue until it was
time to strike."[6]

So don't act too quickly—and don't wait too long. Wait
until the moment of opportunity ripens—then *act*.

Patience with Others—and Yourself

During my first year with the Spartanburg Phillies, I had the
time of my life. We didn't have a great team, but I had fun.
Our manager was Moose Johnson, a fun-loving guy with a

positive outlook. He was eager to try anything, and I enjoyed working with him.

The following year, Moose moved up to become a scout for the Phillies, so we brought in a new manager, Bob Wellman. That year, our team improved dramatically, and we had a fantastic season. But I was miserable! I had no energy, no appetite, no pep. Finally, Mr. Littlejohn took me to lunch. "Pat," he said, "tell me what's bothering you."

I didn't want to talk about it, but finally Mr. R. E. dragged it out of me: I was getting crushed by Bob Wellman. Physically imposing, at 6' 4" and 270 pounds, Bob was intimidating to work with. He was a great manager but a negative human being. He complained about everything—the talent of the players (which was top-notch), the condition of the ballpark (freshly renovated), the team bus (in sparkling condition), the promotions I invented (nothing short of brilliant). Nothing was good enough to suit Bob. I took it personally, and my spirit was getting hammered into the ground like a railroad spike.

The day after that lunch meeting with Mr. R. E., he called Wellman up to his office for a heart-to-heart talk. After that, the situation instantly improved. Bob's complaining stopped, and my life got 1,000 percent easier. Fact is, I don't think Bob even realized how negative he sounded. He never intended to make things hard on me. Negativity was just his style—but Mr. R. E. talked him into trying a more positive approach. Long story short, Bob took Mr. Littlejohn's advice and my job became fun again.

Mr. R. E. had a great way of talking to people that also solved problems. In all the years I knew him, I never heard him say a critical word about any other human being. As far as I know, he never met a person he didn't like. He was genuinely patient and positive toward everyone he knew. I never forgot that—and I always tried to follow his example.

It's not easy being patient with other people, is it? You may have an overbearing boss, an annoying coworker, a difficult parent or an intrusive neighbor. People like that can really test your patience. As someone once said, "Patience is something you admire in the driver behind you but despise in the driver in front of you." And yet, as Mr. Littlejohn told me on more than one occasion, "God has been so patient with me. How can I not be patient with other people?"

So be patient with people's mistakes and failures. Take time to really listen to their hurts and problems. Be patient with human frailties and imperfection; forgive others as you want to be forgiven. Patiently accept people who are different from you. And above all, patiently give people that word of affirmation and encouragement they need.

For a short course in demonstrating patience toward other people, I offer this advice from Bill Marriott, Jr., the chairman and CEO of Marriott Hotels International:

> The six most important words: "I admit that I was wrong."
> The five most important words: "You did a great job."
> The four most important words: "What do you think?"
> The three most important words: "Could you, please?"
> The two most important words: "Thank you."
> The most important word: "We."
> The least important word: "I."

Finally, while you're practicing being patient toward other people, practice being patient with yourself. St. Francis de Sales (1567-1622), Bishop of Geneva, once said, "Have patience with all things but chiefly have patience with yourself. Do not lose courage in considering your own imperfections, but constantly set about remedying them. Every day, begin the task anew."

Patience in Trials

On December 8, 1995, 43-year-old French journalist Jean-Dominique Bauby suffered a massive stroke and went into a coma. Twenty days later, he awoke and found himself almost completely paralyzed due to severe damage to his brain stem. With effort, he could move his head slightly, make a faint sound deep in his throat and blink his left eyelid. The rest of his body was completely unresponsive. His mind was fully active but trapped in a useless body—a rare condition known as "locked-in syndrome."

When his hospital caregivers realized he was aware and fully conscious, they taught him to communicate by fluttering his left eyelid. A translator was brought in to help Bauby communicate. The translator would read letters from an alphabet, with the most common letters listed first, and Bauby would blink when the correct letter was spoken. In this way, he built up complete sentences, letter by letter.

Trapped in a corpse-like body, Bauby made up his mind that he would record his observations and leave them to the world in the form of a book. Once Bauby was able to make his wishes known, a Paris book publisher hired freelance editor Claude Mendibil to work with him throughout the summer of 1996, helping him record and edit his thoughts.

In March 1997, Jean-Dominique Bauby's book, *Le Scaphandre et le Papillon* (published in English as *The Diving Suit and the Butterfly*), appeared in bookstores—a 130-page memoir consisting of 28 short chapters, written entirely by eye-blinks. The book soared to the top of the bestseller lists and won glowing reviews.

Bauby lived just long enough to know that his book was a triumph. Two days after the first copies appeared in the stores, Bauby died of heart failure at age 44.

The book is touching, funny, sometimes angry but never bitter or self-pitying. Those who had followed Bauby's writing career said it was his best work ever. The title of the book came from the fact that at times his existence was like being plunged in a diving suit to the ocean depths of depression, while at other times he felt his mind roam free like a butterfly.

Writing of his physical condition, he wrote, "In the past it was known as a 'massive stroke' and you simply died. But improved resuscitation techniques have now prolonged and refined the agony."

Yet, writing of the butterfly-like freedom of his mind, he observed, "There is so much to do. You can wander off in space or in time, set out for Tierra del Fuego or for King Midas's court." At one point, he imagined being visited by Empress Eugénie, wife of the last monarch of France. He described her yellow-ribboned hat, her silk parasol, her white gauze dress and the scent of her perfume. She came to his bedside and said to him, "There, there, my child, you must be very patient."

And he was patient—amazingly, painstakingly patient as he communicated his thoughts and his experience to the world, blink by blink by blink. As his body, like a diving suit, sank inexorably through an ocean of suffering toward death, his mind took flight like a butterfly. It was patience that set him free.

Brother Lawrence (1610-1691) was a French Carmelite monk and the author of the Christian classic *The Practice of the Presence of God*. He prayed that God would send him pain and tribulation so that he could learn patience and develop greater endurance. Though I know that "tribulation worketh patience" (Rom. 5:3, *KJV*), I have never had the courage to pray for tribulation. Even so, it's good to remember that whenever problems and obstacles arise and it seems that God is trying our patience, He is actually using these experiences to increase our character and enlarge our souls.

Cornelia "Corrie" ten Boom (1892-1983) was a Dutch Christian who, along with her family, helped many Jews to escape Nazi-occupied Holland during World War II. As she recorded in her autobiography, *The Hiding Place*, she and her family were arrested by the Nazis and imprisoned at the notorious Ravensbrück concentration camp. Corrie's sister died at Ravensbrück, but Corrie herself was released in December 1944 due to a clerical error. The week after her release, all of the other women in the camp who were the same age as she were executed.

Corrie used to tell a story to explain how she learned to patiently wait on God, even in times of tribulation. When she was a little girl in Holland, her father would take her on train trips. She would always beg him to give her the train ticket to hold and look at while they were waiting in the station for the train. But her father would only place the ticket in her hands in the final moments before they boarded the train.

The lesson Corrie learned was that her father would never give her the ticket too early or too late. He would always give her the ticket precisely when she needed it. Reflecting on that experience, she realized that God, her heavenly Father, was the same way. He was never late and He was rarely early. God was always on time. His schedule didn't always fit her impatient schedule, but she invariably discovered that His schedule was better than hers. So she learned to ask God for the patience to listen for His voice and to discern His timing for the events in her life.

As pastor-author Charles Swindoll has said, "Waiting goes against human nature. We like to hurry and so we want God to hurry too, but He doesn't. God prepares us during times when the whole world seems to be going on without us. He patiently, deliberately, steadily molds us in the shadows, so we might be prepared for later years, when He chooses to use us in the spotlight."

John Croyle is the founder of Big Oak Ranch, a center for abused and orphaned children in Gadsden, Alabama. In his book *Bringing Out the Winner in Your Child*, he tells the true story of a father who took his two young children for a river ride on a pontoon boat. The father's attention was focused downriver when the motor chugged to a stop.

"Dad," his son called out. "Sherry fell in the water!"

The father looked over the side—and there was his daughter, trapped underwater with her red sweater tangled in the propeller. Her face was less than 12 inches under the surface, and her eyes gazed up into his. Her cheeks were puffed out as she held her breath. She was waiting for her dad to do something.

The father went over the side and tried to free the girl, but nothing worked. He came to the surface, took a gulp of air, then went under, pressed his lips to hers and blew the air into her mouth. Three more times he went up for air, then went down and tried to free his daughter, sharing his air with her as he worked. On one of his trips to the surface, his son gave him a knife, which he used to cut the sweater off the girl.

Finally, the father lifted his daughter into the boat. She was cut and bruised from the propeller, but alive. He took her to the hospital to be checked. There a nurse asked the girl how she had managed to survive.

"Daddy always taught me never to panic when there was danger," she said. "I knew my daddy would come get me."

That kind of attitude is the key to so many of the problems, crises and trials we face: Don't panic. Don't hurry. Take time to think it through and find a solution.

Above all, be patient.

Chapter 3

Pay Your Dues
(You Need to Have Experience)

In 1966, the Spartanburg Phillies had one of the best seasons of any minor league club. Our attendance topped 173,000 fans, breaking all previous records, and we brought home a championship. For the second season in a row, I was named Executive of the Year by the league—and my hat size swelled to triple digits. I just knew the major league teams would soon be bidding for my services.

Within days of the close of that season, my phone rang—and sure enough, it was the Philadelphia Phillies owner himself, Bob Carpenter. As soon as I heard him say, "Pat, this is Bob Carpenter," I knew what was coming next: He was going to make me general manager of his major league baseball franchise! And why not? I had proved I was ready!

But as he began to explain why he was calling, I groaned inwardly. He wasn't offering me the job of running the Phillies organization. In fact, his plans for me were (to my immature thinking) strictly bush league: He wanted me to head up a brand-new double-A farm club in Reading, Pennsylvania. I was insulted! Didn't he realize what I had accomplished in two short years in Spartanburg? Why should I leave a successful gig in Spartanburg to build a team from scratch in Reading? Here I was, ready to run a big league team, and Mr. Carpenter wanted to send me to Mudville! Who did he think he was talking to?

The truth is, I should have been honored, not insulted. Bob Carpenter was expressing enormous faith in me, offering me command of a brand-new start-up operation after only two years on the job. My immature pride clouded my thinking. I agreed to meet with Mr. Carpenter and his front office staff—but I had no intention of taking the assignment in Reading.

The Phillies flew me to Philadelphia for the big meeting. During the flight, I thought about what a big shot I was, being flown all the way to Philadelphia at the team's expense just so I could turn down their offer! When I strode into the Phillies' executive offices, everyone was there: Bob Carpenter (who was not only team owner, but a longtime friend of my dad's), Ruly Carpenter (Bob's son and also my boyhood pal from Wilmington), general manager John Quinn (whose job I felt entitled to), farm director Paul Owens, and several other executives in the organization.

"Pat," Mr. Carpenter said with a warm, welcoming smile, "we're all very impressed with the progress you've made in Spartanburg." He proceeded to lay out the plan for the new team in Reading.

When he had finished, it was my turn to speak.

Digging a Hole with My Mouth

"To be frank," I said, "I don't see how this would be a good career move for me. I'm getting ready to move up to the big leagues. Why should I jeopardize my career by moving to Podunk, Pennsylvania? How do I know it's really a baseball town? Why should I risk everything I've accomplished in Spartanburg by taking this job in Reading?" For the next 15 minutes, I proceeded to dig a hole with my mouth—all the way to China.

As I talked, Mr. Carpenter's expression turned to a cold glare. If I didn't want the job, I could have easily replied with a gracious "thanks, but no thanks," I could have said that I felt obligated to honor my commitment to Mr. R. E. for the 1967 season. But no! I had to be a big shot and toss it back in their faces.

When I got back home to Spartanburg, Mr. R. E. greeted me with a wounded expression. "Pat," he said, "what did you say to Mr. Carpenter?"

"What do you mean?"

"They called me and told me they've cut off your health benefits. Mr. Carpenter always spoke so highly of you, Pat. Now he's furious with you. What did you do?"

"I turned down the Reading job."

"You *what*?" Mr. Littlejohn's face sagged. "Oh, Pat, this is terrible—and I suppose it's partly my fault. I had you so sold on the idea that you could go straight to the big leagues from Spartanburg that you didn't see what an opportunity they were offering you. Pat, the job in Reading was a sign of how much they believed in you, and you should have been honored to take that job." He sighed. "Well, I have to take some of the blame—but, Pat, you have to admit that you handled this thing very badly."

"Yes, sir," I said weakly. "I did that all right."

A few weeks later, Bob Carpenter's son, Ruly, came to see me. As we sat down to talk, he said, "You and I have been friends for years, and you were always a level-headed guy! You made a complete fool of yourself at that meeting. What in the world got into you?"

I could only shrug.

The fallout kept coming. *Sporting News* passed me over for an award everyone expected me to get—the Outstanding Minor League Baseball Executive of the Year award. To my stunned amazement, the award went to an executive whose accomplishments didn't come close to mine. Then it hit me: The editors had probably consulted with the Phillies' brass before making their selection. My arrogance in Philly had undoubtedly cost me that award.

"What Have They Been Feeding You?"

At Christmastime, I visited my mom in Wilmington. While I was there, Mr. Carpenter called and asked me to come over to his home in Wilmington for a talk. Squadrons of butterflies fought dogfights in my belly as I drove to his house. I had known Bob Carpenter practically all my life. He had given me my start in baseball, sending me to the Miami farm club as a catcher, fresh out of college. And I had walked right into his office and insulted him to his face.

He met me at the front door, polite but reserved. It was all I could do to meet his eye and shake his hand. He ushered me into his study and wasted no time in getting down to business.

"Pat," he said sternly, "tell me one thing."

"Yes, sir?"

"What have they been feeding you down there in Spartanburg?"

I gulped hard. "Excuse me?"

"You used to be a decent, well-mannered young man. What happened to you, Pat? You're not the same guy I sent to Spartanburg two years ago."

I shook my head. "Mr. Carpenter," I said, "I know I made a fool of myself, and all I can say is—I'm sorry."

He accepted my apology, but the damage I had done could not be undone. I had ruined my chances of advancing within the Phillies organization.

I learned a painful, valuable lesson: Don't get cocky. Don't expect to run the world at age 26. A few early accomplishments don't mean that the world is going to beat a path to your door. If you keep proving yourself, success will come to you when you're ready.

But first you have to pay your dues.

The 11-Year-Old Mill Worker

When I think of paying dues, I think of Mr. Littlejohn. He was born in the little town of Cross Anchor, South Carolina. His father worked at a succession of jobs, making very little money. Because the family struggled financially, Mr. R. E.

got his first job when he was 11 years old, working in a mill after school and all day long during the summer.

With the money he made as an 11-year-old mill worker, Mr. R. E. was able to buy his own Model T Ford (he paid in cash). He maintained the car himself and drove it around town. One time, when his dad needed to go to the neighboring town for a job interview, 11-year-old Richard Littlejohn drove his dad in the Model T he had bought with his own hard work. Mr. R. E. once told me about that trip.

"Along the way," he said, "we must have had 10 or 11 flat tires. Back then, you didn't buy a new tire when you had a flat—you just put on a patch and pumped it up again. By the time we got to the next town, one of the tires was completely shot—it wouldn't take one more patch. So we had to buy a new tire.

"As it happened, the tire blew right in front of a house where two girls were sitting on the front porch. The girls watched while I changed the tire. They didn't talk to me, and I didn't talk to them. But after my father got a job in that town, we moved into the house across the street from those two girls. One of them was named Marion, and years later, in 1935, I asked her to be my bride, and she said yes."

Mr. R. E. attended Furman University for two years at a cost of $350 a year. At the end of his second year, his savings were depleted, so he went to work as an accountant. Then he tried sales for a while, selling gasoline station equipment—compressors, pumps, hoses, nozzles, and so forth. He went from station to station and sold his wares out of the trunk of his car.

With the beginning of World War II, Mr. R. E. saw a new opportunity open up. Wartime regulations prevented petroleum companies from hauling their own products and required them to use common carriers, so he got into the petroleum-hauling business as part of the War Emergency Cooperative Association. The co-op began with 15 leased tanker trucks.

After the war, Mr. Littlejohn continued in the fuel-hauling business. He even perfected and patented a trailer design that prevented leakage. His fleet grew to more than 650 trucks transporting more than $10 million of fuel per day. Because of his business acumen, he was also named director of the biggest savings and loan company in the county.

When I met Mr. Littlejohn in 1965, he was operating six separate businesses, plus the Spartanburg baseball club (which he co-owned from 1946 to 1974). He was an intensely community-minded leader and was involved in the Boy Scouts, the Fellowship of Christian Athletes and the First Baptist Church of Spartanburg. Though he only attended Furman University for two years and didn't graduate, he generously endowed scholarships and served on the university's board of trustees. He achieved all of this by paying his dues.

When Mr. Littlejohn's two sons-in-law, Bobby Pinson and Jimmy Ballew, went into business with him, they didn't start out in a nice air-conditioned office. They started in the repair shop, wearing overalls and working under tanker trailers, getting covered with grease while learning the business from the ground up. When those young men eventually made it to the executive suite, they knew a side of the business they never could have learned by sitting behind a desk. Mr. Littlejohn made sure that his sons-in-law paid their dues.

My mentor, Mr. R. E., was a wealthy, successful, influential business leader—but he never would have gotten where he was if this 11-year-old Carolina boy hadn't been willing to start at the bottom, work hard and pay his dues. So I ask you: What are you willing to do to achieve your goals? Are you willing to pay your dues in order to live your dreams?

"Where's My Shortcut to the Corner Office?"

When my eldest son, Jimmy, got his master's degree in sports administration at the University of Massachusetts, we had a talk about his future. I suggested some career steps to consider. For example, he might think about group sales with the New Jersey Nets or community relations with the Baltimore Orioles. But Jimmy didn't like those ideas.

As we talked, I got the sense that he would have taken the NBA commissioner's job if it was offered. He was disappointed when I informed him that David Stern probably wasn't ready to retire just yet.

My daughter Karyn was just as ambitious as Jimmy, but her passion was gospel and country music. In February 2001, she won the Miss University of Florida pageant, and in June, she was first runner-up for the Miss Florida title. After the pageant, she was offered a chance for a recording contract—but it meant she'd have to move to Nashville, work on her music during the day and wait tables at night. Karyn would have to pay her dues—but she didn't want to do that. She wanted to be Faith Hill, and she wanted it now!

I explained to Karyn that Faith Hill didn't become a star overnight. She got her start in the music business on the lowest rung imaginable--stuffing envelopes for Reba McIntyre's fan club. "If you want to achieve what Faith Hill achieved," I said, "you've got to pay your dues, just as she did. You've got to stuff envelopes and wait tables. You've got to learn your profession from the ground up."

"But I don't want to stuff envelopes," she said. "I don't want to wait tables. I want to be on stage! I want to make records!"

"Well, tell me, Karyn," I said, "who should step aside to make room for you?"

She had no answer for that one.

"There's only one way to the top," I said, "and you have to pass through each of the lower levels to get there."

Karyn couldn't accept that, so she stayed in Orlando. She dropped out of college at the start of her senior year and soon found herself at a desk, answering phones for a real estate office. And she was miserable.

One day, she received an email with a quotation by architect Carl Bard: "Though no one can go back and make a brand new start, anyone can start from now and make a brand new ending." Those words jolted Karyn's thinking. She realized that she wasn't chained to that desk. She could still make choices about the direction of her life.

In the fall of 2003, Karyn returned to the University of Florida to get her degree in radio and communications. Once she completed her degree, she decided to go to Nashville. She was embarking on her own Pursuit, a dream of a singing career.

She came to me and said, "Daddy, you were right. I'm going to do whatever it takes to fulfill my dreams. I'm going to live in somebody's basement, wait tables, stuff envelopes, sing backup and pay my dues."

I've had the same conversation with most of my kids, with young people in the Magic organization and with the youth in the audiences I speak to around the country. Again and again, I encounter newly minted college grads, with the ink still wet on their diplomas, and they want to run the world. They ask, "Where's my shortcut to the corner office? C'mon, I've been in the mailroom all week! When do I get to be CEO?"

I tell them the same thing Mr. R. E. would say: "You need experience, and you can get the experience you need right where you are. Don't be so impatient. Don't expect the world to beat a path to your door. Pay your dues." They don't want to hear it, but I tell them anyway. If you want to reach the pinnacle in sports, entertainment, publishing, academia, politics, business, or any other field of endeavor, you've got to start at square one. You've got to pay your dues.

Robert Half, founder of Accountemps, said, "An MBA's first shock could be the realization that companies require experience before they hire a chief executive officer." John Bianchi, CEO of Frontier Gunleather, maker of collector-quality holsters and gun belts, said, "I feel sorry for people who didn't climb to the top but jumped there. They miss so much. They miss the challenge of it all. They jumped from kindergarten to graduate school."

Journalist Maria Shriver is a niece of the late president John F. Kennedy, and the wife of California Governor Arnold

Schwarzenegger. After earning her B.A. in American Studies at Georgetown University, she began her career as a broadcast journalist with KYW-TV in Philadelphia. Then she worked as co-anchor of the CBS Morning News in 1985, and eventually moved to the NBC television network in 1987. She took an unpaid leave of absence from NBC when her husband ran for governor in 2003.

She talked about the need to pay your dues (even if you are a Kennedy) in her book *Ten Things I Wish I'd Known Before I Went Out into the Real World*:

> Listen: You can't short-circuit the learning process. It takes time to get to the top, and that's good— because by the time you get there, you'll have learned what you need to know in order to stay there.
>
> So relax, take your time, and don't be in such a rush. And remember: No job is beneath you. But also know that on your way up, you may run into critical and judgmental people, jealous people—people who may say you got where you are because of who you are or what you are, what school your father went to or what you look like or who you knew when. No matter. Shake it off. If they have a problem with you, it's their problem, not yours. Just shelve your ego, put your head down, and bulldog forward, grinding it out. There is no better way to gain respect—and self-respect—than through hard work.[1]

That's good advice: No matter who you are or how far you intend to go in your chosen profession, be willing to start at the bottom and learn as you go. Harold Geneen (1910-1997) was the longtime CEO of ITT and later founded MCI Communications. He once observed, "In the business world, everyone is paid in two coins: cash and experience. Take the experience first. The cash will come later."

Gravel-voiced sportscaster Jack Buck (1924-2002) was the play-by-play announcer for the St. Louis Cardinals. He once said, "You can't do the job until you have some experience, and you can't get experience until you have a job. When I started as a sportscaster at WOSU [the Ohio State University radio station], I had never done a sports show before. When I did a basketball game, it was the first time I ever did play-by-play. It was the same with football. I didn't know how to do those things. I just did them. The way to improve is to keep doing it, getting as much experience as possible. That's still true today."

One of the best ways to gain experience is by interning. An intern position doesn't pay very much—and in some businesses, interns aren't paid at all. But that's often the only way to get some bona fide experience to put on your résumé. Even if you can't get a job without experience, you can usually get an internship—and that's where you get the experience to land a job.

While my son Thomas, one of my South Korean sons, was working on a double master's at Seton Hall University in New Jersey, he got an internship in the business office of the New York Yankees in 2004. He did so well that they brought him back for a second-year internship in the hopes that a full-time job would open up for him. The job didn't happen—but Thomas was able to land a third-year internship with the Boston Red Sox. At the end of the 2006 season, a full-time job opened up for Thomas—and he was on his way. Thomas paid his dues.

My son Bobby went into the Cincinnati Reds farm system right out of college and spent five years coaching minor league baseball. He later moved to the Washington Nationals farm system and in March 2007 was named Farm Director for the Nationals. You don't get to be an executive in the big office without spending a few years in the hinterlands. Bobby paid his dues and is now reaping the rewards. Mr. Littlejohn would have liked that.

Experience Teaches the Teachable

During my third season in Spartanburg, I decided to top the promotions we had done during the previous two years. One of our biggest promotions involved personal appearances by celebrity sports stars like NFL quarterback Bart Starr. Celebrities don't work cheap, and I spent Mr. Littlejohn's money like it was nothing. We had a set budget for promotions, but I busted that budget like a sledgehammer smashing a watermelon.

Mr. R. E. saw that I was over-spending like a madman, but he didn't say a word. We had blowout attendance—and we should have cleared an enormous profit. But I was so promotion crazy that I completely forgot about the bottom line.

I had a clause in my contract that stated I was to be paid a percentage of the profit. That was my incentive to hold the line on expenses. Because of the expense of my promotions, my year-end bonus was a fraction of what it would have been—and I had only myself to blame.

Why did Mr. R. E. let me spend promotion money like there was no tomorrow? He wanted me to gain *experience*. He was tracking the numbers and he knew exactly what was coming—but he let it play out so that I could learn an important life lesson. That shrunken bonus check taught me far more than any lecture he could have given me.

I paid my dues that year—and I paid 'em in real dollars.

Experience, they say, is the best teacher. Unfortunately, people are not always good learners. Experience can't teach you anything if you are not teachable. Frederick the Great, King of Prussia from 1740 to 1786, put it this way: "Some are incapable of learning from experience. In my army there are pack mules that have been through seven military campaigns. That is a great deal of experience—but they are still pack mules."

Someone has said that "experience" is simply the name we give our mistakes. There's a lot of truth in that. Mistakes and failures are often the very learning experiences we need. Novelist Victoria Holt said, "Never regret. If it's good, it's wonderful. If it's bad, it's experience." But we don't automatically learn from our mistakes and experiences. We have to make the effort to understand *why* we made a mistake, *why* we had a particular experience.

Aldous Huxley observed, "Experience is not what happens to a man. It's what a man does with what happens to him." Experience doesn't truly become a *learning* experience until you reflect on it, analyze it and understand it. Lorraine Moller is a marathoner from New Zealand who has competed in four summer Olympics. She says, "I treat everything as a learning experience. Then I become detached from the result and more interested in the experience itself." And golfer Tiger Woods puts it succinctly: "You should learn something from each and every round you play."

Permit me to quote a few wise sayings on the subject of *experience*. Then tell me if you don't identify with these sentiments:

- "Education is when you read the fine print. Experience is what you get if you don't" (singer-songwriter Pete Seeger).

- "If we could sell our experiences for what they cost us, we'd all be millionaires" (columnist Abigail Van Buren).

- "Good judgment comes from experience, and experience often comes from bad judgment" (writer Rita Mae Brown).

- "Experience is something you don't get until right after you need it" (actor-comedian Steven Wright).

- "Life is a succession of lessons which must be lived to be understood" (poet Ralph Waldo Emerson).

Do I hear an "Amen"?

While researching my book on the life of Walt Disney, *How to Be Like Walt*, I was fascinated to learn of his early business experiences. His first venture, Laugh-O-gram Films, Inc. of Kansas City, went bankrupt when Walt was 21 years old. Unable to pay the rent for his apartment, he lived out of a cardboard suitcase, sleeping on the couch at his office. Once a week, he rented a bathtub, towel and soap for a dime at the railroad station. In the bankruptcy judgment, the court allowed Walt to keep one movie camera and one can of film. All the other assets were seized to pay the creditors.

In July 1923, a financially washed-up Walt Disney left Kansas City by train and headed for a new life in California. In his suitcase were two shirts, two sets of underwear and a can of film. His pancake-thin wallet contained $40 in cash—the proceeds from the sale of his movie camera. He was determined to start his life over again in the movie capital of the world.

"I was twenty-one years old," he later recalled, "but I had failed. I think it's important to have a good hard failure when you're young."

Coach Lou Holtz agrees. "Everyone should experience defeat at least once during their career," he said. "You learn a lot from defeat." And NBA star-turned-senator Bill Bradley observed, "The taste of defeat has a richness of experience all its own."

When we experience a defeat in life, we tend to focus only on the pain. We feel humiliated and embarrassed. We reproach ourselves and wallow in self-pity. We forget to look for the lesson in our experience of defeat. Editor and writer Peter DeVries once said, "We all learn by experience, but some of us have to go to summer school." And poet Archibald McLeish agrees: "There is only one thing more painful than learning from experience and that is *not* learning from experience."

A *smart* person learns from his experience—but a *wise* person learns from the experience of others. One of the wisest people I know, pastor Andy Stanley of North Point Community Church in Alpharetta, Georgia, once said, "Experience is a good teacher, especially if it is other people's experience. There's no point in learning something the hard way if someone else has already paid that price."

So be wise. Learn from the experiences of others as well as your own. It's important to pay your dues, but it's foolish to pay more than you have to.

Some Tips for Dues-payers

Writer Laura Ziv has some advice for those whose careers aren't progressing as quickly as planned and who are getting tired of paying—and paying and paying—their dues:

> *Your vision:* A corner office with a panoramic view, a six-figure salary, a fat expense account complete with a generous clothing allowance and a gleaming limousine to ferry you to and from the office . . . all, of course, before you hit thirty.

> *Your reality:* A cubicle the size of a bathroom stall, a paycheck that gets chuckles from the bank teller when you cash it, and a bus ride (with two transfers) to get you home . . . and the big three-oh is coming at you like a bat out of hell. What happened?

While there is nothing wrong with a good dose of ambition, bear in mind that "it is extremely rare to reach the apex of your career in your 20s or 30s," says Jan Yager, Ph.D., a sociologist and workplace expert and author of *Friendships* (Hannacroix Creek Books, 1997). "Every career has a path, and you should be aware of what yours is for your industry. Whatever field you're in, there is a certain amount of information you must absorb, both academically and experientially, before you reach the top. It's called *paying your dues.*"[2]

Here are some tips to help get you through the dues-paying stage of your life as you pursue your dreams and goals:

1. *Set clear goals for your life.* Type up your goals in big letters, post them where you will see them daily and review them often. Don't shove your goals into a drawer and forget them. You might wake up someday and find that, instead of paying your dues, you've been spinning your wheels. Keep your mind on The Pursuit. Stay focused on your goals.

2. *Pay your dues cheerfully.* Always display a positive, eager attitude. Be ready for promotion and advancement—but while awaiting your big break, show your boss that you have a team attitude.

3. *Be proactive and assertive.* Opportunities rarely fall into your lap. You have to pursue them. Young people often come to me and say, "Mr. Williams, I'm eager to get ahead in the sports business. Here are my goals. How would you advise me to reach for them?" I've never felt

that such a question was pushy or out of line. I respect ambition, and I always try to lend a hand to anyone who asks that question.

4. *Don't expect your first few jobs to be fulfilling.* "Paying your dues" means doing the things you'd rather not do in order to work your way up to your dream job. Your entry-level job isn't supposed to be fulfilling. It's meant to be a starting point. Maria Shriver put it this way: "Starting at the bottom is not about humiliation. It's about humility—a realistic assessment of where you are in the learning curve." Fulfilling work will come in time. For now, seek your fulfillment in outside interests—spiritual pursuits, leisure activities, hobbies, friendships and relationships.[3]

5. *Be courageous and persistent.* Eleanor Roosevelt said, "You gain strength, courage, and confidence by every experience in which you really stop to look fear in the face." You must face life with courage and persistence. Don't let anyone discourage you or intimidate you. Don't let any obstacle stand in your way. Be relentless and unstoppable in the pursuit of your goals. Adopt the long view of life. Don't expect shortcuts or lucky breaks. Most successful people make their own luck over the long haul by persevering through obstacles and setbacks. The way to suc-

cess is usually a ladder, not an elevator, so keep climbing—and you'll get there.

6. *Be flexible.* If you try to put your career on a rigid timetable, you'll set yourself up for discouragement and frustration. No one's life moves in a straight line. You have to flex in response to life's zigs and zags. Keep adjusting to changing circumstances and keep moving forward.

7. *Speak well of everyone.* Never bad-mouth the boss or your fellow employees, even after you leave a place of employment. Spreading negativity helps no one—and could come back to bite you. Even if your experience was negative, stay positive. Keep your words soft and sweet because the day may come when you have to eat them.

8. *Adopt a learner's attitude.* While paying your dues, keep growing and improving yourself. Read books, take courses and develop new skills. Continually seek new ways to make yourself a more valuable member of the team.

As I write these words, I'm 67 years old. My kids and coworkers are often surprised when they hear me say that, at my age, I'm still paying my dues. When my staff lines up a speaking engagement for me, I'll sometimes say, "Oh, that will be a good experience for me. That will build up my résumé and help me get to the next level."

They look at me like I'm nuts! They say, "Build up your résumé? You're almost 70! Isn't it time for you to retire?"

I just laugh and say, "Are you kidding? I'm *always* building my résumé! I'm *always* trying to get better at everything I do! That speech you just booked for me is six months away, right? Well, by the time I give that speech, I will have given 75 other speeches, read 200 more books and collected 500 more stories to use in my speeches. I'll be a *much* better speaker by then than I am today."

You see? If you approach life with the right attitude, you never stop learning, growing and improving. You never stop gaining experience. You just keep gaining more and more mastery of your craft as long as you live.

It's one of the hardest lessons I had to learn at "Littlejohn University," and it's a lesson that often falls on deaf ears in this "I want it now!" world we live in: You can reach your goals—but first you have to pay your dues.

Chapter 4

Keep It Simple

During my four years in Spartanburg, Mr. Littlejohn and I had an annual ritual. New Year's Day is a big event in the South. Every year, Mr. and Mrs. Littlejohn would have me over for a traditional New Year's Day supper in which every item of food had a symbolic meaning.

The entrée was succulent roast pork, which symbolized health. Turnip greens were reminders of dollar bills, and black-eyed peas represented coins, which together symbolized prosperity. Mrs. Littlejohn would add rice and gravy, slices of ripe cantaloupe and Southern-style sweet iced tea for good measure. After the meal, Mr. R. E. and I would watch the bowl games on TV, after which I would usually fall asleep on their sofa.

There was another ritual that Mr. R. E. and I observed every New Year's Day. That was the day we negotiated my salary for the coming year. Those negotiations were unlike any bargaining sessions I've been involved in before or since.

Mr. R. E. had a simple way of conducting these sessions that he called a "paper swap." We would each have a piece of paper. He'd have me write on my piece of paper the dollar figure I would like to be paid. At the same time, he'd write down what he proposed to pay me. Then we'd exchange papers. The amazing thing was that his number always topped mine. As you can imagine, that simplified the negotiation process tremendously. We always went with his number.

He paid me so well that I was able to drive a big Oldsmobile Toronado and wear expensive suits. I saw myself as a successful young executive, and I wanted my clothes and my ride to express an image of success. Mr. Littlejohn was tolerant of (and amused by) my flashy style and the airs I put on.

Though Mr. R. E. was vastly more successful than I pretended to be, his personal style was simple and humble, not flashy in the least. He liked to have everything as simple as possible. He enjoyed simple foods, maintained a simple lifestyle, communicated in simple words and lived by a simple philosophy.

Mr. Littlejohn believed that life should not be complicated. "Keep it simple, Pat," he often told me. "We have a tendency to make things more complicated than they really are. Let's just keep it simple."

I remember going to meetings with him and laying out my plans for him with charts, projections and rows and rows of figures. He'd say, "Now, Pat, I'm just a country boy. I don't have a big fancy Master's degree like you. I don't drive a big Olds Toronado like you. Could you put all this in terms that I can understand?"

Again and again, in various ways, he continually taught me to keep it simple.

Is there a goal that you wish to accomplish? State it simply so that you can keep it in mind. Is there an idea that you wish to convey to others? Express it simply so that people can grasp it at a glance. Do you have a plan to present to your team, company or organization? Make it a simple plan that everyone can buy into.

Clear Out the Clutter

"Our life is frittered away by detail. Simplify, simplify." So wrote Henry David Thoreau at Walden Pond in 1854. More than a century later, that's still excellent advice.

Bestselling author Elaine St. James is the leader of the simplicity movement. "It takes time to make time," she says. "You can't figure out how to create time for the things you enjoy if you don't take time to rethink what you're doing now. Maintaining a complicated life is a great way to avoid changing it."

In 1990, St. James was a busy real-estate investor, author and seminar speaker who lectured on real estate investing. She worked 12-hour days, lived in a high-maintenance mansion and rarely saw her husband (who maintained as hectic a schedule as she did). St. James was staggering under the stress of her out-of-control schedule, but she couldn't see any way out of her complex, high-pressure lifestyle.

Gradually, it dawned on Elaine St. James that she had a choice—she could change her lifestyle. She got rid of material possessions that cluttered her house and her life.

Then she and her husband moved to a smaller house near his office, eliminating his four-hour round-trip commute. After making those changes, St. James discovered that she and her husband had magically added an additional 30 hours to each week. "It's hard to put a price tag on that much time," she concluded.

This discovery gave birth to a whole new career. She began speaking and writing about how we can all simplify our lives. Her bestselling titles include *Simplify Your Life: 100 Ways to Slow Down and Enjoy the Things That Really Matter* and *Simplifying Your Life with Kids: 100 Ways to Make Family Life Easier and More Fun*.

"Simplifying your life," she says, "is really about gaining control of your life—creating more time, on the job and at home, to do the things you want to do. All the surveys I've seen reach the same conclusion: More and more people feel that they aren't spending their time on things they enjoy. A *Time*/CNN poll found that 65 percent of people spend their leisure time doing things they'd prefer not to do. That's staggering! What's the point of leading a 'full life' if you don't have the time and energy to enjoy it?"[1]

What keeps us from simplifying our lives? Simply this: We have too much stuff! We are choking on our own affluence. And when the stuff we have ceases to satisfy, we go out and buy *more* stuff. We are constantly spending money, including money we don't have, and digging ourselves deeper into debt while renting storage space so that we can have a place to stuff our stuff.

Is that insane or what? Why are we working ourselves into an early grave, chasing after possessions we really don't need and would be happier without? Our relentless drive to acquire and consume is one of the great sicknesses of our culture. Someone has even given that sickness a name: *affluenza*. The Old Testament writer of Ecclesiastes saw that the disease of affluenza, of striving to acquire wealth and possessions, was ultimately meaningless. He called it "chasing after the wind" (Eccles. 4:4).

Tammerie Spires was a management consultant with the accountancy firm of Price Waterhouse. She lived in Dallas, enjoyed her job and was happy with the big money she made. But soon after her two children were born, she realized that she was missing something. She wasn't happy with corporate life anymore. Though her company offered her a big raise to stay with the company, she opted for the life of a full-time mom. Now her family lives on her husband's salary—and she has a life she really wants.

After leaving the corporate world, she made a fascinating discovery. "I realized I was passionate about camping," she says, "so I wrote a book called *A Guide to Happy Family Camping*, and it got published. My great dream of writing a book would never have come true if I hadn't stopped believing in what other people defined as success and started looking for what *I* defined as success."[2]

Many in corporate America, both men and women, are forsaking the affluence rat race, forgoing the big money and mega-stress of the fast-track world in order to simplify their lives. They are downsizing their cluttered lives and donating truckloads of stuff to the Salvation Army. Many are trading in their ostentatious homes for a low-maintenance lifestyle. Some are telecommuting or taking up home-based businesses.

In the process, they are discovering that the simple things in life bring the greatest joy and contentment. It's all about time spent with family and friends, time spent in fellowship with God, time spent enjoying life and discovering life's deepest meaning. If we want to experience rich and rewarding lives, we need to clear out the clutter and simplify, simplify!

Diane Clark and her husband, Craig, live on a single salary—Craig's income as a public school teacher. They have found that they can live an adventurous life, taking long, exotic vacations that most people only dream of—and they do so by traveling on a budget. "We back-packed through England, France, Spain and Italy with our biggest expense being a bargain airfare and rail pass," Craig Clark said.

Many people find that the pathway of simplicity leads to a deeper connection with God. "We are Christians," said Diane Clark, "and I think simple living is kind of a natural growth toward spirituality. We can spend more time on what is important. Christians, of all people, should be less materialistic. Simplicity is not depriving yourself of things and activities; it's about having a richer life, enjoying what you already have and making do with what you have."[3]

Elaine St. James, Tammerie Spires, Craig and Diane Clark—these are just a few of the people who are living the life Thoreau described from the edge of Walden Pond. He urged us to engage in The Pursuit, to "live deep and suck all the marrow of life." But Thoreau's call to pursue the adventure of life is above all a call to simplicity. "Go confidently in the direction of your dreams," he wrote. "Live the life you've imagined. As you simplify your life, the laws of the Universe will be simpler."

Simplify Your Business Life

I was 28 years old when I moved to Philadelphia to begin my career in the NBA. The year was 1968, and my boss was Irv Kosloff, a tough-minded paper magnate who had bought the Syracuse Nationals in 1963 and moved them to Philly, renaming them the Philadelphia 76ers. Irv was a street-smart businessman and though I saw him as a mentor, I also found him very intimidating. Whenever I met with him to report on the operation of the team, I would try to present as much good news as possible in order to stay in Irv's good graces.

Irv could see right through me. He saw how I was killing myself trying to micromanage every detail while straining to put a positive spin on everything, including my failures and mistakes. So, early in my first year with the 76ers, Irv Kosloff sat me down and gave me some good advice. "Pat," he said, "every morning when you start your day, just ask yourself two simple questions: What am I doing to help the team win more games? And what am I doing to sell more tickets? Your job here is really no more complicated than that." That was sound advice, and I never forgot it.

In the previous chapter, I told you about my son Thomas, who is 25 years old and paying his dues in the sports management arena. As a senior accountant with the Boston Red Sox, he goes to work every day at Fenway Park. I recently asked him, "Thomas, with what you've already learned, could you run a major league ball club?"

"Yeah, Dad," he said, "I think I could. All you have to do is sell some tickets, take care of the fans and win some ballgames. There are more details, of course, but that's pretty much all there is to it."

I had a good laugh over Thomas's answer, and it occurred to me that Irv Kosloff and Mr. Littlejohn would have gotten a kick out of that answer, too. At an early stage in his career, Thomas has learned an important lesson in business and in life: Keep it simple.

In business, less is more, and simple is better than complex. If you're writing a marketing projection, a business plan, a sales report or a press release, reduce it to its most basic elements. If you can't distill your ideas and information down to a single 8.5 x 11 sheet of paper, then your plan or report is too complicated. Simplify! The best answers are always the simplest ones. Complexity baffles the mind. Simplicity liberates the imagination. As Walt Disney often said, "Keep it simple, so a child can understand it."

The life of Rich DeVos, the cofounder of Amway, is a great American success story. I first met Rich in August 1990. The Orlando Magic did not yet exist, and I was working with several Florida business leaders to bring a major league baseball franchise to Orlando. At a crucial juncture in the process, our ownership group collapsed. We needed to find a new owner quickly and obtain a hefty cash infusion. A friend of mine set up a meeting with Mr. DeVos, and I flew to Michigan to meet with him.

Now, everyone knows that you never go into a business meeting without a lot of charts and graphs and market analyses and feasibility studies. But I had no time for all of that. I went to Michigan with one piece of paper torn from my notepad. On that sheet, I drew a circle with some crisscross lines—a crudely drawn pie chart. The chart illustrated in simple terms the various shares of each investor in the ownership group, including the share that we hoped Mr. DeVos would purchase.

My meeting with Rich DeVos lasted less than 40 minutes. I presented my chart and made my pitch. He listened attentively, and then he said, "Excuse me—I'll be right back." He left the room for three or four minutes, then he returned, shook my hand and said, "Tell the league we'll go forward with them."

He had just made a $95 million decision.

That decision eventually led to Rich DeVos becoming an owner of the Orlando Magic—and a good friend of mine. I framed that piece of paper, which hangs on my office wall, tangible proof of the power of simplicity.

Roger Dow, vice president and general sales manager for Marriott Lodging, once made an eye-opening discovery of the value of simple solutions for complex business problems. He once asked the information technology department at Marriott to consider ways to enable the computer program to recognize repeat customers. The experts studied the problem and reported that it could be done—at a cost of $4 million over three to four years.

Roger Dow abandoned the idea as being too costly and complicated.

A few weeks later, Dow traveled to Southern California and checked into the Marriott in Irvine. Dow had stayed there before, and he exchanged greetings with the doorman, who knew him by name. Then Dow passed through the lobby and approached the registration desk. The young woman at the desk smiled and said, "Welcome back to the Marriott. It's good to see you again."

Dow was surprised. He had a good memory for faces, yet he didn't recall this woman. "Have we met before?" he asked.

"Well," she replied, "probably not. Actually, I only started working here three weeks ago."

"Then how did you know that I'm a returning guest?"

"Oh," she said, "that's simple! I worked out a signal with the doorman. When guests arrive, he takes their bags and says, 'Have you ever stayed here before?' And if they say yes, then he looks at me and tugs on his ear lobe to let me know."

It was a simple solution to a seemingly complex problem—and it didn't cost $4 million and four years to implement. If you want to be successful in business, always look for the simplest solutions.[4]

You've probably eaten lip-smackin' ribs at Famous Dave's Legendary Pit Bar-B-Que—but did you know that the founder, Dave Anderson, is a Native American and an enrolled member of the Chippewa and Choctaw tribes? Or that Dave earned a Master's degree in Public Administration from Harvard University without earning an undergrad degree? Or that from 2003 to 2005, Dave served as Assistant Secretary of the Interior for Indian Affairs? And you thought he just made outrageously good ribs!

Dave Anderson started the first Famous Dave's barbecue shack on the outskirts of Hayward, Wisconsin, in 1994. From that one humble restaurant, Famous Dave's quickly became a chain that spread across the country. What is the secret of Famous Dave's success? The answer is simplicity itself.

"As long as people are eating three times a day," he says, "there is going to be a need for great food. So where can you go? The answer is really simple. How many backyards in America have a barbecue grill? We are America's food. We are barbecue ribs, we are barbecue chicken, we are coleslaw, potato salad, honey-buttered cornbread. That's simple, but it's really good eating.

"The idea for Famous Dave's comes from the backyards and neighborhoods of America, from the simple backyard barbecue. So we have a very simple concept. We have a real simple menu. Our training is very intense, but it's simplified. It's a training we call 'Three Step Simple.' We built our whole training program around things that are simple. And so when we put this thing together to franchise across the street corners of America, we made a commitment to keep everything simple. We kept our menu simple, we kept our training simple and we kept our focus simple. Because of that, customers like to eat here and investors know that Famous Dave's is a company that can grow, and it can go into any community because it's about great food and simplicity of operation."[5]

Keepin' it simple. That's the secret ingredient in Dave's success. Take it, use it and cook up some simple success of your own.

Simplify Your Game Plan

No matter what sport they compete in, the great coaches and players know this: The key to winning is simplicity. Vince Lombardi, the legendary coach of the Green Bay Packers, used to say, "I believe in simple things done with consistent excellence rather than complicated things done poorly." He continually preached simplicity to his Packers. "Football is a simple game," he told them. "It is, first, getting the ball off your own goal line and, second, getting it across your opponent's goal line."

Michelle Akers is a retired professional soccer player. She won a gold medal in Atlanta as a member of the 1996 U.S.A. Women's Soccer Team. Her winning philosophy: "The best players do the basic, simple things perfectly, every time, and under the most pressure."

Bill Vukovich was an American racecar driver and widely considered one of the greatest drivers in the history of American motor sport. He won the Indianapolis 500 in 1953 and 1954, and was in the lead during the fity-seventh lap of the 1955 Indy race when he was killed in a chain-reaction crash. After winning his second Indy 500, a reporter asked him the secret of his success. His reply: "There's no secret. You just press the accelerator to the floor and steer left."

The game of basketball looks complicated. It's a fast and highly competitive game. In pressure situations, when time is running out and the players are nearing exhaustion, who is most likely to win? The team with the simplest game plan.

Former UCLA coach John Wooden was a master at coaching in high-pressure situations. He would call a timeout, gather his team around him and calmly diagram the play. It was always a scheme that his players had practiced repeatedly and could execute in their sleep. "It's a simple game," Coach Wooden reflected, "and coaches tend to foul it up and complicate it. I wanted to keep it very simple."[6]

The late Al McGuire coached the Marquette University men's basketball team from 1964 to 1977. He was inducted into the Basketball Hall of Fame in 1992. "Basketball is simple," he once said. "You just take this round ball, put it up and through the hoop and then get back to the other end of the court on defense before the other team gets there. That's the game! Simplify. Make it easy. Go out and play basketball!"

George Karl is head coach of the Denver Nuggets and currently twelfth on the all-time win list for NBA coaches. "I think basketball is over-analyzed and over-scrutinized," he told *USA Today*. "It's played the best when it's played simple, when there is a rhythm and an intuition and togetherness. . . . We make it out to be brain surgery, and it isn't. I just believe in good basketball players playing with each other."[7]

Coach Charlie Spoonhour has coached basketball at Southwest Missouri State University (now Missouri State University), St. Louis University, and the University of Nevada, Las Vegas (UNLV). He recalls a lesson he learned from an opposing coach when he was a high school coach:

> In the waning seconds of a very close game, Spoonhour watched in baffled amazement as the opposing coach called a timeout—then said absolutely nothing to his players. The entire team sat on the bench throughout the timeout—and they simply stared at their shoelaces. Then the horn sounded— and before the players could get to their feet, the coach called *another* time out. Again, he said not a word—no motivational speech, no diagramming of plays on his clipboard. Just silence and staring at the floor.

At first, Spoonhour wondered what was going on across the court—and then the realization hit him. "He had them thinking about what they should be doing," Spoonhour said.

The horn sounded again—and those players came out on the court and battled hard. They executed brilliantly. Those players didn't need words. They didn't need a pep talk. They just needed to settle down, focus, and remember everything their coach had taught them in practice. The coach had learned that the key to winning was to keep it simple—and Coach Spoonhour learned that lesson as well.

"When I was a young coach," Spoonhour recalled, "I'd try to tell [my players] fifteen things. Now, I say one or two things and save my breath."[8]

The message is clear: Do you want to achieve your goals? Do you want to win? Then simplify, simplify!

Simplify Your Communication

If you've been to a New York Yankees home game anytime in the past six decades, you've undoubtedly heard the voice of Bob Sheppard, the public address announcer for Yankee Stadium since 1951. In his long career (interrupted by a stint as a naval gunnery crew commander during World War II), he has announced 4,500 major league baseball games and 22 World Series. Bob is famous for his refined announcing style, which he honed as a speech teacher (Yankee slugger Reggie Jackson calls him "the Voice of God").

When my wife, Ruth, and I were cowriting our book on public speaking, *Turn Boring Orations into Standing Ovations,* I interviewed Bob by phone—his telephone voice was so much like his stadium voice that I could almost hear the echo as he spoke. I asked Bob to share with me the keys to being a good public speaker, and he replied, "The keys to being a good public speaker are the same as the keys to announcing a game at Yankee Stadium: be clear, be concise, be correct."

I thought, *Mr. Littlejohn would have liked that very much.* How simple and succinct: Be clear, concise and correct. That's the essence of effective communication, effective leadership and effective living.

Do you want to communicate effectively? Do you want to communicate for success? Then simplify your spoken and written communication. Get rid of jargon, doubletalk, technospeak, psychobabble and grandiloquent (big) words.

Take a lesson in communication from General Eisenhower. In 1945, Nazi Germany had just surrendered, and the war in Europe was over. At Supreme Allied Headquarters in Reims, France, General of the Army Dwight David "Ike" Eisenhower presided over a meeting of his staff. The purpose of the meeting was to compose a telegram to the White House, officially announcing the historic event. Eisenhower's patience wore thin as his aides tried to out-do each other with flowery verbiage and purple prose.

Finally, Eisenhower took pencil and paper and quickly dashed off a single sentence. Then he cleared his throat and read it to his staff: "The mission of this allied force was fulfilled at 0241 local time, May 7, 1945." The message was sent. It was classic Ike—dignified, direct and simple.

Another famous figure from World War II was Britain's prime minister, Winston Churchill. He, too, appreciated simple communication. He once said, "All the great ideas are simple and many can be expressed in a single word: freedom, justice, honor, duty, mercy, hope."

Churchill once received a massive report prepared by a junior minister of the government. Without even peeking under the title page, he pushed the stack of pages away. "This report," he said, "by its very length, defends itself against the risk of being read."

Veteran sportscaster Dick Enberg recalled a lesson he learned the day of his first major league broadcast for the Angels. "I was up in the booth," he said, "and I was so excited and anxious to get started. Fred Haney, the Angels general manager, came into the booth and said, 'Let me give you the key to announcing: Report the ball. If you follow the ball, it will always lead to the action.' Simple advice, but I've never forgotten it."

My friend John Maxwell, motivational and leadership guru, made this profound observation about the value of simple, direct communication:

There is great dignity in simplicity. Most of the immortal works of literature not only have the brilliance of brevity but also the dignity of simplicity. The Lord's Prayer consists of only fifty-seven words, none more than two syllables. The Declaration of Independence, which revolutionized the thinking of the entire world, can be read by a fourth grader in less than five minutes. Simplicity is eloquent. It speaks loud and clear, without insulting the intelligence of the listener.

Then there's Lincoln's immortal Gettysburg Address, consisting of just 272 words, more than three-quarters of them words of one syllable.

Do you want to communicate with impact? Do you want your message to move and persuade people? Then simplify, simplify!

A Simplicity Checklist

It has been said that "living simply" means making the journey of life with *just enough* baggage—and no more. So let me offer a few suggestions for making your journey through life a little easier and lighter:

1. *Simplify your schedule.* If you are feeling stressed and burdened by too many responsibilities and demands on your time, it's time to streamline your priorities. "No one can maintain more than three priorities," says Elaine St. James. "If you have a job you care about, that's a priority. If you have a family, that's a priority. Which leaves one more. Maybe it's staying in shape, maybe it's volunteering at your church—but that's it. Most people understand this intuitively. But they keep overcommitting themselves and overcomplicating their lives."[9]

2. *Clean out the clutter.* If you're living like a pack rat, it's time to shovel out your home or office and start living like a human being. Make your life livable by cleaning out the clutter. Make room for things that matter and hang on to meaningful mementos—but do you really need that Reagan-era bowling trophy on your fireplace mantle? At least once a year (say, every St. Swithun's Day!), go through your house and toss out every item you haven't used in the past year.

3. *Think twice about purchases.* Before you buy that gadget, ask yourself, "Will this purchase simplify my life—or complicate it?" Elaine St. James suggests putting prospective purchases on a "Thirty Day Wait List." After deferring the purchase for 30 days, if you still want it or need it, then go ahead and buy it. Odds are, however, that after 30 days you will probably change your mind—and that will save both money and clutter. Even if you choose to buy that new lamp, leave on the price tag for a week and save the receipt. You may decide to take it back to the store.

4. *Put extra time in your life.* Practice keeping phone calls short. Find ways to simplify meal preparation and cleanup. Move closer to your workplace and reduce your commuting time. Get up an hour earlier and work on that novel you've always wanted to write. With a little imagina-

tion, I'm sure you can find many ways to add hours of quality time to your life.

5. *Turn off and tune out.* Unplug your TV. Put away the video games. Spend more time exercising, reading, traveling, learning and doing the things that really matter in life.

6. *Practice saying no.* Sometimes family members and other people will impose on you, stealing time that could be better spent working toward your goals. It's okay to say no to people who impose on you. Sure, it's important to give back to the community and volunteer and support worthy causes, but make sure you prioritize your activities and keep your life simple. When people make unfair demands on your time, it's okay to say, "Sorry, I'm booked." You don't need to explain or make excuses. If people don't respect your firm, polite refusal, you're not being rude—they are. As playwright Jules Renard once said, "The truly free man is he who can decline an invitation without giving an excuse."

7. *Remember that "simple" doesn't always mean "easy."* President Ronald Reagan was once accused of offering simplistic solutions to complex problems. He replied, "There are simple answers. There just aren't any easy ones." Sometimes simplifying our lives is a very hard thing to do.

> It often requires determination and effort to
> take the most simple and direct action.

It is a fairly simple matter to unclutter our living space, to give away possessions we don't need, to control our spending, to end phone calls sooner, to stop watching so much TV and to say no to pushy people. It's all so incredibly simple—but it's not easy. We don't want to let go of our useless stuff. We don't want to control our spending or give up our couch potato ways. We're not comfortable saying no to people, even when they are rude and demanding. These solutions are simple, but they're not easy.

So simplifying our lives may be a hard thing to do—but let's face it: Everything worth doing is hard. It takes thought, determination, discipline and effort. But the rewards of living simply are nothing short of amazing.

For years, I've done a weekly sports interview show in Orlando. One of my favorite guests was the late Joe Falls, longtime Detroit sports columnist. One day, near the end of our interview, Joe said, "Pat, you want to know the key to success?"

I said, "Sure, Joe! What is it?"

"Two things: Enjoy your life and be good to people."

That was a nice, simple way to end the show—and it's a nice, simple way to end this chapter.

Chapter 5

Don't Run from Your Problems
(They Give You an Opportunity to Sell Yourself to Others)

I think a minor league baseball team is the number-one problem attractor in the world. Whatever can go wrong will go wrong—and it will usually go wrong on the biggest night of your season. Power failures, cloudbursts, plagues of locusts—these are just a few of the things that can put a crimp in your game night festivities.

One of the most important duties of a minor league general manager is promotion. During my years in Spartanburg, I was constantly trying to cook up new ways to attract people to the park. One of my favorite promotions was an idea I came up with in 1966. The Phillies organization sent us two pitchers out of spring training, John Parker and John Penn. Well, those names were too perfect to pass up! We had to have a Parker-Penn night.

I contacted the Parker Pen Company in Janesville, Wisconsin, and ask them for some freebies to give away at our Parker-Penn night. They shipped us cartons of their famous pens, and we promoted up a storm. But even before the big Saturday night in Duncan Park, the problems began to multiply.

We tried to book our musical entertainment for the evening to fit the Parker-Penn theme—and who else but the fabulous Ink Spots? We tracked them down and invited them to perform "If I Didn't Care" and other classic hits at Duncan Park. Unfortunately, they were already booked to sing at Mickey Mantle's Holiday Inn in Joplin, Missouri.

A few days before the game, John Parker got called into the Army. We had lost Parker, but we still had Penn—or so we thought. On Saturday morning, John Penn's wife gave birth and he informed us he would not be at the game that night. So no Parker, no Penn. To top it all off, the biggest thunderstorm in the history of Spartanburg rolled in that night, and the entire game was washed out.

We rescheduled the promotion, and when game night finally arrived, John Parker got a weekend pass, John Penn arrived with his wife and new baby, the weather was beautiful and everything went off without a hitch.

During my years in Spartanburg, I would often go to Mr. Littlejohn with a list of problems and say, "What should I do? How should I solve these problems?"

He'd always say, "Don't run from your problems, Pat. This will give you a wonderful opportunity to sell yourself to the community" or "This is your big chance to show the brass in Philadelphia what you can do." I just wanted to get the problems off my plate and out of my way, but Mr. Littlejohn saw them as selling opportunities.

If you are lounging around on satin sheets with your head on a silk pillow, a box of bonbons by your side and roses at your feet, you may think you're living the good life—but you won't have a chance to prove your worth as a problem solver. But if all your plans blow up and you suffer opposition and adversity, then you will have the opportunity of a lifetime. Everybody around you will be watching to see what you do next.

Will you blow up? Will you melt down? Or will you astound the world with your brilliance as a problem solver? This is your big chance, my friend. What are you going to do with it?

Face and Embrace Your Problems

Our natural human inclination is to avoid problems. We even avoid *thinking* about problems. We ignore them and hope they'll go away—but problems rarely go away on their own; they usually only get worse.

It seems counterintuitive, but instead of running *away* from our problems, we should run *to* them. If we *face* our problems, *embrace* our problems and *solve* them, we'll show the world what we're made of and what we can do. It takes courage to face our problems and character to embrace our problems. I've never known a problem solver who didn't possess these traits.

Here's the great paradox of life and its problems: If you expect life to be easy, you will have problems. But if you expect problems as a natural part of life, you will have a life of adventure.

We all wish our problems would get in line and take a number so that we could solve them one at a time. But problems are unruly. They come at the most inopportune times. They mob us and scream at us, demanding our attention. That's just the way life is, and we need to adjust our expectations accordingly. Psychiatrist Theodore Rubin put it this way: "The problem is not that there are problems. The problem is expecting otherwise and thinking that having problems is a problem."

People often prefer to put up with a painful but familiar problem rather than expend the effort to find a solution. Many people will endure a throbbing toothache for months just to avoid spending half an hour in the dentist's chair. You can't be successful in life by turning your back on your problems. You must face them and solve them.

In his short story of the sea, *Typhoon*, Joseph Conrad wrote of Captain MacWhirr and his young chief mate, Jukes, who stood on the deck of the steamer *Nan-Shan*, steering into the teeth of a killer storm. As the waves and spray washed over the two men, threatening to sweep them overboard, the Captain told Jukes, "We must trust her to go through it and come out on the other side. . . . Keep her facing it. . . . The heaviest seas run with the wind. Facing it—always facing it—that's the way to get through."[1]

And another old man of the sea, Admiral William "Bull" Halsey, commander of the U. S. Third Fleet in the Pacific during World War II, said, "All problems become smaller if you don't dodge them, but confront them. Touch a thistle timidly and it pricks you. Grasp it boldly and its spines crumble."

Sometimes people rationalize and say, "It's not my problem. Why should I solve it?" They see an injured man lying on the sidewalk, and as they step over him, they think, *How awful for that poor man. Why doesn't anybody help him? Somebody ought to do something.* It never occurs to them to think, *I'm somebody. I should do something.*

I once heard Rick Warren, author of *The Purpose-Driven Life*, speak at a business breakfast in Orlando. I scribbled three napkins-full of notes as he talked.

"Life is a series of problems," he said. "The reason we have to deal with problems in life is that God is more interested in our character than our comfort. He is more interested in making us whole than He is in making us happy. He wants us to grow in our character and become more like Christ.

"Everyone in this room is either going into a storm, is in the middle of a storm or is coming out of a storm. Everyone has problems. I used to think that life was a series of mountains and valleys—mountaintop highs and valley lows. But I don't believe that anymore.

"I believe that life is kind of like two rails on a railroad track. Most of the time you have good things and bad things in your life all at once. No matter how good things are, there's always a problem that needs to be faced. No matter how bad things are, there's always something good to thank God for.

"This year I've gotten royalties of $30 million for my book *The Purpose-Driven Life*. At the same time, my wife is battling cancer. See what I mean? There's the problem-free track and the problem track, and both are going on at the same time. We have to learn to deal with both tracks simultaneously."

This is a powerful insight into the true nature of life. It's rare that we ever get to take a vacation from our problems. Even in times of great blessing, there are difficulties we must deal with. We have to be thankful for our blessings at the same time we are facing and solving our problems.

Problems: The Key to Advancement

As I was starting my first season in Spartanburg, it became apparent that the Phillies front office had a huge problem with a key employee. Talking to other managers in the Phillies farm system, I could tell that everybody was as aware of the problem as I was. In fact, the buzz around the system was that if the problem wasn't solved, the entire organization would be harmed by mass resignations.

I was concerned—not only because the problem affected my job in Spartanburg, but also because Bob Carpenter, the Phillies owner, was a longtime friend of the family. I sat down with Mr. Littlejohn and told him about the problem. "What should I do?" I asked.

"Pat," he said, "in fairness to Mr. Carpenter, you should go to Philadelphia and explain the situation to him. Problems don't go away when you ignore them. They only get worse."

So I took Mr. Littlejohn's advice. I flew to Philly for a meeting with Mr. Carpenter. Even though Mr. Carpenter was an old friend, it was an intimidating experience for me to walk into the boss's office and tell him about a major problem in his organization. But I did it.

After I told Mr. Carpenter what was happening and who was responsible, he shook his head and said, "Why am I always the last one to know?" The problem was going on right under his nose, yet he hadn't heard a thing about it. If I hadn't laid out the situation for him, he might not have known until it was too late.

Mr. Carpenter thanked me and said, "I know it couldn't have been easy for you. I'm grateful for your candor."

As I flew back to Spartanburg, I thought about the valuable lesson I had learned from Mr. Littlejohn: Don't run from problems. Face them, embrace them, solve them—then get on with your life.

If you want to advance in your career, if you want to be noticed and promoted, then be a problem solver. Business writer Brian Tracy puts it this way:

> If I asked you what you did for a living, you would tell me the name of your current position or job description. Whatever your title, your real job is 'problem solver.' This is what you do all day long. It is this ability that makes you valuable. You are a professional problem solver. Your success in your career is determined by how effectively you solve the problems and achieve the goals of your position.[2]

Problems are your ticket to advancement. When Edward Cole was president of General Motors, an interviewer asked him, "What makes you different from other men? Why have you moved ahead of thousands of others and achieved the top job at General Motors?" Mr. Cole replied, "I love problems." And leadership guru John Maxwell said, "Those who master problem-solving find that it's one of the fastest ways to attain a leadership position in any group. Anyone who can solve problems will never lack influence."

As Mr. Littlejohn drilled into me, again and again, problems give you the chance to sell yourself. "I'm grateful for all my problems," reflected James Cash Penney, founder of the J. C. Penney department store chain. "As each of them was overcome, I became stronger and more able to meet those yet to come. I grew on my difficult things." And industrialist Henry J. Kaiser pointedly said, "I always view problems as opportunities in work clothes."

Legendary NBA referee Dick Bavetta holds the record for most games officiated in a career that goes back to 1975. He was the ref who ejected 10 brawling players during an infamous Knicks-Nuggets game in December 2006, and he also raced former NBA star Charles Barkley for charity at the 2007 NBA All-Star Weekend.

Dick recently told me a story about the importance of not running from problems. In the early 1980s, he was a young ref who had been tapped to officiate a game between the Philadelphia 76ers and the Celtics at Boston Garden. The game occurred during my tenure as general manager of the 76ers (1974 to 1986), though I wasn't present at that game. Looking back, I wish I'd been there to see it, because it was a night to remember.

In those days, there were only two refs on the court, and Dick's partner was veteran referee Jack Madden. It was a raucous crowd and an intense game. Early on, Jack Madden collided with a Celtics player, went down and broke his leg, and had to be carted off the floor. Dick Bavetta would have to work the rest of the game by himself.

Dick called the two coaches together, Billy Cunningham of the 76ers and K. C. Jones of the Celtics. "Let's get along, fellas," Dick said. "Let's cooperate." Dick told me that the spirit of cooperation lasted about 20 seconds.

Before long, there was total chaos on the court. Everything that *could* go wrong *did* go wrong. Dick had to charge K. C. with a technical foul. Then he looked in the corner and saw Julius Erving of the Sixers and Larry Bird of the Celts choking each other. He ejected both superstars. Then he charged Billy Cunningham with a technical and tossed him out of the game. While Billy headed into the tunnel to the locker room, he was mercilessly pelted by Celtics fans.

No sooner had Billy left the court when the scorer's table told Dick that Billy had only received one technical, not two—so Dick erred in ejecting him. Bavetta got Billy out of the locker room and as Billy was coming out of the tunnel, he got another pelting from the rowdy Celtics fans.

The game rumbled down to the final buzzer and, mercifully, it was over. Dick thought his career was over as well. He was sure there had never been a more chaotic, out-of-control game in the history of the NBA.

The next day in the Boston newspaper, Billy Cunningham praised Dick Bavetta for having the guts to throw out the two stars, Erving and Bird. That commendation from the Philadelphia head coach caused NBA officials to take notice of Dick Bavetta. No longer was he viewed as a rookie, but as a battle-seasoned pro who made tough, fair decisions in the midst of a crisis. "That was the turning point of my officiating career," Dick told me. "I started getting choice assignments because the league started looking at me as a leader."

The moral of the story? All the problems Dick Bavetta dealt with during that one wild game provided the pivotal moment of a Hall of Fame refereeing career. Those problems gave Dick a chance to sell himself.

That's the lesson Mr. Littlejohn was teaching me: "Don't run from problems, Pat. They give you a chance to sell yourself." When he said those words to me, I wasn't sitting in a classroom. I was in the trenches, and problems were being fired at me from every direction. I advanced in the sports business by proving I was a problem solver. Now, more than 40 years later, I'm carrying that same message to the next generation.

"Houston, We Have a Problem . . ."

Apollo 13 lifted off on April 11, 1970, carrying three men—Commander Jim Lovell, Command Module Pilot Jack Swigert, and Lunar Module Pilot Fred Haise. Their destination: the Moon. They would never reach their destination. Two days into the mission, while the spacecraft was in orbit around Earth, Jim Lovell radioed those now-famous words, "Houston, we have a problem . . ."

Lovell and his companions had more than a problem. They had a full-blown crisis. An oxygen tank had exploded, crippling the spacecraft. Power levels dropped. Precious oxygen bled into space. The onboard computer failed. The ship was in a slow, out-of-control tumble. No one on the ground or in orbit understood what caused the crisis—and no one had any solutions.

At Mission Control, flight director Gene Kranz assembled his crisis management team. They quickly laid out what little information they had. The spacecraft was 200,000 miles out in space and moving away from Earth. The astronauts' only hope was a "free return" trajectory, a loop around the moon that would bring the ship back to Earth. But Apollo 13 was off-course, and if the ship's course couldn't be corrected, it would keep sailing on toward deep space.

The crew of Apollo 13 shut down systems to conserve oxygen and power. Lovell and Haise tried to maneuver the ship into the return trajectory, but the controls were sluggish, the ship wobbly. Lovell finally got the ship oriented and fired the engine. Soon they were back on trajectory—but their problems were far from over.

The life-support system of the command module was failing, so Lovell, Haise and Swigert went through a connecting hatch into the lunar module. It had enough air, water, and heating power to keep two men alive for 45 hours. Somehow, it would have to support three men for twice that long. And there was more: Apollo 13 would have to make one more course correction without help from the computer—and no one had any idea how it could be done.

As Apollo 13 approached the shadow of the moon, Houston scientists came up with an idea of aligning the spacecraft's attitude by sighting on the sun with the spacecraft's telescope. It wouldn't be very accurate, but it just might be close enough for government work. Lovell handled the controls while Haise eyed the sun through the telescope's protective filter. Lovell fired the engines—and the maneuver worked.

To conserve energy, the astronauts shut down all power, plunging the ship into total darkness. As they drifted in the dark, another problem arose—a potentially lethal buildup of carbon dioxide. The lithium hydroxide filters that removed

CO_2 from the air of the lunar module were nearly spent. There were fresh filters in the dead command module—but they were square, not round like the ones in the lunar module. It appeared that the astronauts would suffocate before the ship ever reached Earth.

Then flight director Gene Kranz informed his team, "Failure is not an option." Once again, Mission Control found a solution to a seemingly insoluble problem. Houston engineers rigged up a makeshift system for filtering out CO_2 using only items that the astronauts had onboard: a plastic storage bag, a notebook cover and gray duct tape. Haise cobbled together the makeshift life support system—and it worked. The solution wasn't pretty, but it saved three lives.

Still, the problems continued to multiply. The temperature inside the spacecraft dropped to a bone-chilling 38 degrees. Water from a leaky dispenser drenched Swigert's feet, leaving them numb from the wet and cold. The men found it impossible to sleep—and almost impossible to concentrate. Exhaustion clouded judgment and eroded patience. Haise became ill with an infection and fever.

It became apparent that Apollo 13 was approaching Earth at too shallow an angle. If the course wasn't corrected, the spacecraft would bounce off the atmosphere and carom back into space. But if the course was over-corrected, the ship would come in too steeply and burn up like a meteor.

Jack Swigert and Fred Haise returned to the abandoned command module. To their amazement, the ship's power and computer systems still functioned. Lovell joined his fellow astronauts in the command module, then they jettisoned the lunar module.

Swigert nudged the controls. *Not too much,* he told himself, *and not too little.* Apollo 13 sank into Earth's atmosphere and became a shooting star, trailing superheated gases.

At Mission Control, communications with the spacecraft blacked out. This was normal and expected. But when the time came for radio communication to resume, there was only static. A full minute passed and hope turned to despair.

Then Jack Swigert's voice crackled over the speakers. Apollo 13 had come home.

Some say NASA's proudest moment was when Neil Armstrong set foot upon the Moon and announced, "That's one small step for man . . ." But I say it was the time Apollo 13 was beset with problem after problem, and NASA found solution after solution until all three heroes came back alive.

Principles for Problem Solving

It is amazing what the human mind and spirit can accomplish once a person decides that failure is not an option. Here, then, are some problem-solving principles to keep in mind whenever you face a crisis of astronomical proportions.

1. Accept Problems as a Challenging Adventure

Taking on impossible odds is crucial to The Pursuit. Life would be boring without problems to solve. Battling adversity enables us to feel truly engaged with the adventure of living. There's a rush of exhilaration that comes when we see life not as a barrage of problems to be endured but as a continual quest for new challenges to conquer. When that is our perspective, the adventure of life becomes a thrill ride.

2. Accept Responsibility for Solving Your Own Problems

In *The Confidence Course*, Walter Anderson wrote, "Bad things do happen; how I respond to them defines my character and the quality of my life. I can choose to sit in perpetual sadness, immobilized by the gravity of my loss, or I can choose to rise from the pain and treasure the most precious gift I have—life itself."[3] What is the problem confronting you right now? Is it a financial calamity? A boss you can't stand? A chronic illness? A goal that seems forever out of reach? Whatever the problem you face, the *real* battle is not "out there" somewhere. The *real* battle is *within you*. The enemy you must conquer is your fear, laziness, avoidance, self-doubt, exhaustion and negative attitude. If you can master the part of you that wants to complain, make excuses or give up, then you can master your problems. Once you accept responsibility for your own problems, you have already begun to solve them.

3. Take Time to Define the Problem

In a 2007 interview with *Investor's Business Daily,* General Colin Powell reflected on the way problem-solving skills are taught in the U.S. military. "What military officers are trained to do," he said, "is solve problems. The first thing you do is make an assessment of the situation. Let the situation dictate what you're going to do. And don't always fall back on what you did previously. I've tried to teach that to my officers and live that example."[4] The moment a problem has been clearly stated and well defined, the solution starts to come into focus as well. It often helps to define the problem in writing. The very process of setting down the problem on paper can be a helpful step in arriving at a solution.

4. Break Big Problems Down into Several Smaller Ones
Many "unsolvable" problems become quite manageable once we break them down into a series of step-by-step solutions. As mathematician René Descartes observed, "Divide difficulty into as many parts as necessary in order to resolve it."

5. Once You Know What to Do, Do It
The best way to get a problem out of your way is to solve it. Don't hesitate. Don't procrastinate. Once you've figured out the solution and know what to do, just do it. Avoiding the problem only prolongs it. Often, the most important step in solving a problem is simply to begin. In the long run, solving a problem takes far less time and energy than trying to ignore it.

6. Maintain a Positive Attitude
It's human nature to focus negatively on the problem—but problem solvers focus positively on the solution. "Go forward confidently," said Norman Vincent Peale, "energetically attacking problems, expecting favorable outcomes." Helen Keller was struck deaf and blind by illness when she was 18 months old. Without sensory input, she grew up like a wild animal. At 7, Anne Sullivan of the Perkins Institute for the Blind took Helen under her wing and taught her to communicate. When Helen was 10, Anne Sullivan taught her to speak. Although the girl was unable to hear, she learned to form vocal syllables after only a month of instruction. At age 24, Helen Keller graduated with honors from Radcliffe and went on to become an author and a lecturer. She faced problems in her life that you and I can hardly

imagine, yet she overcame them all with a positive attitude. "Be of good cheer," Helen Keller once said. "Do not think of today's failures, but of the success that may come tomorrow. You will succeed if you persevere, and you will find joy in overcoming obstacles."

7. Avoid Superficial Fixes to Deep-rooted Problems

Anthony J. D'Angelo, founder and chief visionary officer of The Collegiate EmPowerment Company, said, "When solving problems, dig up their roots instead of just hacking at the leaves." Problems that have only been superficially "fixed" tend to come back later—and more vexing than ever.

8. Accept the Fact that Problems Are Inevitable

In *The Road Less Traveled*, M. Scott Peck put it this way: "Life is difficult. This is a great truth, one of the greatest truths, because once we truly see this truth, we transcend it. Once we truly know that life is difficult—once we truly understand and accept it—then life is no longer difficult. Because once it is accepted, the fact that life is difficult no longer matters."[5] It's human nature to want to escape our problems, especially when they reach the boiling point. We think, *This problem is beyond human endurance,* or *I can't take one more day of this.* But the truth is that we can do whatever we have to do in order to solve our problems. We can endure far more than we imagine. We can achieve far more than we dream possible. But first we have to accept the great truth that life is difficult and problems are inevitable. There's no point in asking, "Is life going to knock me down?" It will. The only question worth asking is, "When life knocks me down, do I have what it takes to get back on my feet and keep moving forward?"

9. Think Outside the Box

This phrase has become such a cliché that people have forgotten what it really means. It simply means that we should seek new, original, creative approaches to solving problems. Let me show you what I mean by posing a riddle: What can you sit on, sleep on and brush your teeth with? To find the answer to this riddle, you have to think outside the box. (Answer to come.) Psychologist Abraham Maslow said, "If the only tool you have is a hammer, you tend to see every problem as a nail." So our goal as problem solvers is to maintain a mental toolbox filled with varied and assorted problem-solving tools. The more innovative our thinking, the more tools we will have for conquering life's challenges. Here are some examples of the kind of tools we need.

Imagination

Imagination is the ability to envision things that do not yet exist. As Rod Serling used to say at the beginning of every *Twilight Zone* episode, "You unlock this door with the key of imagination." A person with imagination knows that in an infinite universe there are innumerable ways to solve a problem, just waiting to be imagined.

Resourcefulness

Resourcefulness is the ability to apply imaginative solutions to difficult problems. An excellent example of resourcefulness was when NASA's Mission Control engineers concocted a life support system out of a plastic storage bag, a notebook cover and duct tape. Resourcefulness solves problems in surprising ways, using whatever resources are available.

If you've ever been to Wal-Mart, you have seen a resourceful solution in action—though you probably didn't realize it. That solution is called a greeter—the person who welcomes you as you enter the store. You may think that the Wal-Mart organization simply wants to appear friendly. But in reality, the greeter serves a pragmatic purpose that affects the company's bottom line in a big way.

In 1980, Wal-Mart founder Sam Walton visited a store in Crowley, Louisiana, that had suffered significant losses due to shoplifting. The resourceful store manager had devised an amazingly simple solution: He hired a greeter to stand at the door and say hello to everyone who entered. Honest shoppers enjoyed the personal touch, but potential thieves took the greeting as a gentle hint that they were being watched. Losses from shoplifting fell sharply after the greeter was hired.

Sam Walton loved the idea and implemented the practice in every Wal-Mart store. It was a resourceful solution that produced huge savings for the nationwide retail chain.

Creativity

Creativity is the ability to think without self-censoring. The creative mind is not hemmed in by such restrictions as "That's the way we've always done it." Creative people are always eager to try the untried, test the untested and invent what has never existed before.

Remember the riddle I asked a few paragraphs ago? "What can you sit on, sleep on, and brush your teeth with?" The answer is so simple that we easily miss it: a chair, a bed and a toothbrush. We assume that a riddle always asks for one answer—but the creative mind wonders, *Why does it have to be one answer? Why not three?* Once we have shattered the "box" of our assumptions, the problem is easy to solve.

Perhaps you feel stuck in life, trapped in a dead-end career or a dead-end relationship. Pastor Rick Warren offers this diagnosis of your problem—and a likely solution:

> I've noticed that when people are stuck in life, it's usually because they're still framing their problem with a set of assumptions that no longer apply. Or they're using the same problem-solving techniques that they used in the past, but those techniques no longer work. You must develop your creativity—specifically your creative problem-solving skills.[6]

Insight

Insight is the ability to see a problem in a penetrating and perceptive way. Insight can't be taught in a classroom, but it can be learned by experience. Over time, we can all develop a knack for making accurate hunches based on fragmentary information. It's the ability to find solutions to problems that defy rational analysis. Sometimes, you just don't have enough information to solve a problem with logic alone. When logic tells you one thing, but your intuition says, "Go with your gut," that's insight.

Humor

Humor is the ability to maintain a clear perspective on problems by not taking them too seriously. In *Jump Start Your Brain*, author Doug Hall makes this observation on the problem-solving power of laughter:

> Hard-core academic research underscores the link between creativity and fun. Alice Isen of the University of Maryland made the point in an article she wrote for *The Journal of Personality and Social Psychology*. She described a study in which two groups of college students were shown two different videotapes, and given a range of creative problems to solve. The first group saw a five-minute clip of bloopers lifted from *Gunsmoke, Have Gun Will Travel*, and *The Red Skelton Show*. The students in the second group watched a math video entitled *Area Under a Curve*. I've never seen this production myself, but I imagine it is every bit as gripping as the title makes it sound.
>
> Guess what? The students in the first group— the ones who'd been laughing and were in a good mood when they took the test—were found to be 300 to 500 percent more likely to come up with successful solutions to the problems they were given.
>
> Stop. Think. Look how easy this is. You can increase your brainpower three- to five-fold simply by laughing and having fun before working on a problem.[7]

Let's face it: Problems make us tense and can even paralyze us. A good sense of humor keeps our brains lubricated so that we can perform at or near our peak, even under pressure.

Obliquity

Obliquity is the ability to view a situation from an oblique or divergent angle. Sometimes the only way to solve a problem is to stop banging your head against it and simply back away. A writer friend of mine says that he gets his best ideas by stepping away from his computer and taking a walk or a nice hot shower. Obliquity is the process of taking your logical cerebral cortex off the problem for a while and letting your subconscious mull it over. Often, when you gain a new perspective on the problem, the solution comes like a bolt out of the blue.

Sky-watchers and astronomers will tell you that you can't see faint stars in the night sky by looking right at them. Why? Because there's a small depression at the center of the retina called the fovea centralis. Weak light does not register there, so to see a faint star, you must look slightly to the right or left of it. In other words, you have to view it obliquely.

It is the same with problems. Sometimes it seems there is a fovea centralis of the mind. Stare directly at the difficulty and the solution eludes you. But move off-center and view the situation from another angle—and the solution comes into focus.

Novelist André Gide (1869-1951) put it this way: "It is not always by plugging away at a difficulty and sticking to it that one overcomes it. Often it is by working on the one next to it. Some things . . . have to be approached obliquely." When facing a problem, keep your mind wide open for new perspectives, creative ideas and oblique ways of thinking. You can't solve a problem with the same kind of thinking that caused the problem in the first place. Your solution lies outside the box.

10. Learn the Lessons of Life's Problems

Even when we face stubborn problems that refuse to change, we can still allow our problems to *change us* by making us stronger, wiser and better human beings. We can always learn the lessons our problems are trying to teach us.

Mr. Littlejohn always seemed happiest when I had a problem to solve. It's not that he took sadistic delight in my misfortunes, but he definitely *enjoyed* watching me wrestle with a problem. He was not just my boss; he was my mentor. He would often say, "Pat, this problem is going to do you a lot of good." He knew that I would learn and grow from the experience of solving that difficult problem.

Mr. Littlejohn was right. Solving problems *was* good for me—and those experiences gave me many opportunities to sell myself. I know for sure that I wouldn't be where I am today without all the problems I had to solve when I was in my twenties.

Years later, when I was general manager of the Chicago Bulls, I had lunch with my pastor, Dr. Warren Wiersbe. I was pouring out a tale of woe about problems in my job. I expected him to sympathize with me. Instead, he gave me this advice: "Now, Pat," he said, "don't waste your sufferings. Life is full of problems, so you might as well put them to good use." I still don't like problems any more today than I did back then—but with the benefit of hindsight, I can see the maturity and character that have resulted from the adversity in my life. Although I wouldn't want to go through those experiences again, I wouldn't trade them for the world.

In the New Testament, we read, "When all kinds of trials and temptations crowd into your lives, my brothers, don't resent them as intruders, but welcome them as friends. Realize that they come to test your faith and to produce in you the quality of endurance. But let the process go on until that endurance is fully developed, and you will find you have become men of mature character, men of integrity with no weak spots" (Jas. 1:2-4, *Phillips*). That's what happens in our lives when we make a conscious decision to learn the lessons of our problems and difficulties. As Benjamin Franklin said, "Those things that hurt, instruct."

There's something to be learned from every problem, so write those lessons down. Preserve your insights for future reference in your personal journal. Don't waste your sufferings, my friend. Wring all the benefits you can from your problems.

When You Find Yourself Being Swallowed by a Snake

Let me share one final story about facing your problems.

One Sunday morning, our pastor, David Uth, was speaking at First Baptist Church in Orlando. When he told this snake story, it got everybody's attention.

When missionaries are assigned to the Amazon River region of Brazil, they are instructed in how to respond if they ever encounter a deadly anaconda snake. Anacondas can grow up to 20 feet in length and can weigh 350 pounds. Despite their size, they move incredibly fast. Missionaries are told, "If you ever encounter an anaconda, do not run. They are faster than you are and you won't stand a chance."

Now, that's a problem. If you can't outrun an anaconda, what are you supposed to do? Remember, don't run from the problem. Face it.

Here's the solution: If you encounter an anaconda, lie down flat on your back. Stay perfectly still. Do not panic. The snake will begin to ingest you, starting at your feet. Let him ingest you up to your knees. Have your knife drawn and ready. Make sure it's sharp. Insert the knife inside the anaconda's jaws, rip upwards, and cut the head off with one smooth motion. And you're out—

Problem solved.

Chapter 6

Pay Attention to the Little Things

One winter while I was working in Spartanburg, I came down with a respiratory flu. The cough hung on for weeks and refused to clear up. Mr. Littlejohn urged me to see his doctor, but being young and indestructible, I said I didn't need a doctor, thanks.

Mr. R. E. called me one day and invited me to lunch to talk over plans for the coming season. We met at a country restaurant in town, but the conversation was mostly small talk. Something was up—but what?

After lunch, I headed for my car, but Mr. R. E. said, "Let's take my car. You can pick yours up later."

So we drove—and Mr. R. E. didn't say a word. When he pulled up in front of his doctor's office, it became clear. I had ignored his suggestion to see a doctor, so he dragged me to the doctor for my own good.

"Come with me, Pat," he said. "Dr. Abel's expecting you." I went in and Doc Abel gave me a good going-over.

He prescribed an antibiotic, and after a week or so, my cough was gone.

A flu bug is a little thing, a submicroscopic organism—but Mr. Littlejohn knew that little things can cause big problems. He often said, "Pat, you got to pay attention to the little things. Those small details that escape your notice will get you every time."

Being in the petroleum hauling business, Mr. Littlejohn had learned that every little detail matters. All he needed was for one mechanic to forget to tighten one lug nut on one wheel, and a tanker trailer could end up overturned in a ditch. So Mr. R. E. was a fanatic about the little things.

"If you're mindful of the little things," he told me, "the big things pretty much take care of themselves."

The Pebble in Your Shoe

Over the years, I've discovered that Mr. Littlejohn's focus on managing the little things is shared by virtually all successful people, in every walk of life. Near the end of his autobiography, *My American Journey*, General Colin Powell lists his "Thirteen Rules," and Rule No. 8 is: *Always check the small things.*

I once spoke to a business group in Orlando, where a woman came up afterwards and handed me her business card. She was a manager for a company in Georgia. On the card under her name, where the job title usually goes, was this statement: "I'm in charge of the little things." I thought, *What an interesting job she must have!* A year later, I spoke to a group in Charlotte, and a man came up and gave me his card—he was the CEO of the same Georgia company. On the card under his name was that same statement: "I'm in charge of the little things." Then I understood: In that company, *everybody*—from the CEO on down—was in charge of the little things.

When I speak to audiences, I often ask, "How many of you have ever been bitten by an elephant?" Never has a hand gone up. So I ask, "How many of you have been bitten by a mosquito?" Every hand goes up. I say, "You see? The little things get you every time."

While researching my book on John Wooden, *How to Be Like Coach Wooden*, I interviewed more than 800 people, including dozens of his former players. Many of them told me about Coach Wooden's annual October tradition. At the first practice of each season, Coach would teach his players how to put on their shoes and socks. The entire hour was spent on how to fit the sock snugly around the heel and toe, how to smooth out the wrinkles, how to spread the shoe, adjust the tongue, tighten the laces snugly at the eyelets, and on and on.

I asked Coach why he devoted so much attention to shoes and socks. He said, "The little things matter. All I need is one little wrinkle in one sock to put one blister on one foot—and there goes my season. I started teaching about shoes and socks early in my career, and I saw that it really did cut down on blisters during the season. That little detail gave us an edge."

The Champ himself, Muhammad Ali, put it this way: "It isn't the mountains you climb that wear you out. It's the pebble in your shoe."

I Can Feel that Groove

What's true in basketball is equally true in every other sport: You have to pay attention to the little things. Woody Hayes coached the Ohio State Buckeyes to 3 national championships, 13 Big Ten conference championships and 4 Rose Bowl appearances. "In football," he said, "the little things are really the big things." Bear Bryant, the longtime head football coach of the Alabama Crimson Tide, said, "Little things make the difference. Everyone is well prepared in the big things, but only the winners perfect the little things."

Hall of Fame NFL coach Vince Lombardi (1913-1970) put it this way: "Football is a game of inches, and inches make the champion." Offensive lineman Jerry Kramer played for Lombardi's world champion Green Bay Packers. He explained the coach's obsession with the little things: "Vince Lombardi pays such meticulous attention to detail that he makes us execute the same plays over and over, a hundred times, two hundred times, until we do every little thing automatically. He works to make the kickoff-return team perfect, the punt-return team perfect, the field-goal team perfect. He ignores nothing. Technique, technique, technique, over and over and over, until we feel like we're going crazy. But we win."

In his book *Red-Hot Cold Call Selling*, Paul S. Goldner says that the little things can quickly add up to a 1,000 percent difference in earnings. He wrote:

> Consider Jack Nicklaus, perhaps the greatest golfer of all time. During one year in the 1960s, at or near the peak of his skills, Nicklaus earned approxi-

mately $400,000 on the PGA tour. There was another golfer on the PGA tour that year as well. His name was Bob Charles. . . . During the same year, Bob Charles earned approximately $40,000 on the PGA tour. The difference in earnings between Bob Charles and Jack Nicklaus was approximately tenfold (excluding income from endorsements and other revenue-generating activities). It might surprise you to learn that the difference in their respective per-round stroke averages was less than half a stroke.[1]

We see the same principle at work in the game of baseball. The late *Chicago Daily News* columnist Sidney J. Harris noted that the little things make all the difference when it comes to batting averages in major league baseball. "One batter hits .275 for the season," he wrote. "The other hits .300. The one who hits .300 may easily have a contract awarding him twice as much money as the one hitting .275. Yet the difference between the two over the season is only one extra hit in forty times at bat."

Whitey Herzog, famed former major league baseball outfielder, coach and manager, put it this way:

Baseball, when it's played right, is made up of a lot of smaller plays, and each one gives you an edge if you work at it. It's also a game of large samples: Over 154 or 162 games, the little things accumulate and pile up and turn into big ones. That's the game's most essential fact. It's a game of percentages, and any way you can tilt the wheel your way a little, you do. Casey [former Yankees manager Casey Stengel] tilted it one degree here, another degree there, till the ball just seemed to roll the Yankees' way and he looked up in August and saw New York right where they always seem to be, at the top of the standings, looking down. Writers and fans hardly ever notice these little things, and you hardly ever hear anybody mention 'em, but they decide championships. No good club ever won a thing without 'em.[2]

Of all my heroes in sports, Ted Williams (1918-2002) tops the list. In 19 seasons with the Boston Red Sox (interrupted by active duty as a Marine Corps pilot), Ted led the league 6 times in batting. He retired with 521 career home runs and a career batting average of .344. He was the last major leaguer to bat over .400 in one season (.406 in 1941).

Jack Batten, the Red Sox trainer from 1950 to 1965, remembered Ted's attention to the little things. "His sweatshirts have to fit just right," said Batten. "He breaks in shoes a year in advance. You've seen him tug and twist a cap. That's to make it fit just so. A poor fit might distract him. He'll rip out a worn shoe lace. Right down to the smallest detail, everything has to be just right. Nothing must interfere. He makes sure of that."

I got to know Ted personally after I moved to Orlando and began attending the induction ceremonies of the Hitters Hall of Fame at the Ted Williams Museum in St. Petersburg. Every February, there would be a ceremony and dinner, and even after his stroke, Ted would attend in his wheelchair.

When Ted entered the room, every conversation stopped and Ted was the center of attention.

I remember at one of these dinners, a fan went to Ted and held out a bat. "Ted, I've had this bat for a long time," he said. "I'm told that you used it in 1941, the season you hit .406."

Ted took the bat and closed his eyes as he worked his hands around the grip. "Yep," he said, smiling and remembering. "Yep, this is one of my bats. In 1940 and 1941, I would cut a groove in the handle for my right index finger to nestle in. I can feel that groove. This is one of my bats all right."

Even after 60 years, for Ted Williams it was still the little things that mattered.

Both a Visionary and a Detail Person

After I moved to Orlando in 1986, I developed a great admiration for Walt Disney. I even wrote two books on his life and philosophy. When Walt was building the world's first theme park in 1955, he said, "The thing that's going to make Disneyland unique and different is the detail. If we lose the detail, we lose it all."

Walt built his career on paying attention to the little things. In 1937, as his first feature film, *Snow White and the Seven Dwarfs*, was nearing release, Walt decided that Snow White's cheeks were too pale. Though he was running out of time and money, Walt ordered his painters to make Snow White blush. The ink and paint artists tried every shade of pink paint they had, but none of them satisfied Walt's eye for detail. Finally, one artist took out her makeup kit and dabbed some rouge onto Snow White's cheeks—

perfect! The rouge was added to thousands of drawings and Snow White's makeover was completed in time for her premiere.

This was just one of thousands of little details that Walt perfected during production. After the release of *Snow White*, the Walt Disney Studio was no longer viewed as "that Mickey Mouse cartoon factory." *Snow White* transformed Walt Disney into one of the most respected and admired filmmakers in the world—because he paid attention to the little things.

What is your "Snow White"? What's the life goal you are pursuing with all your might? A business career? An athletic achievement? A career in the arts or entertainment business? A career in academia? Public service? The military? The ministry? Whatever your Pursuit, my friend, whatever the trajectory of your career, pay attention to the little things.

You may say, "But I'm not a detail person. I'm a visionary. I see the big picture. I'm a creator, an entrepreneur, a leader. I don't need to pay attention to the little things. When I'm running the show, I'll hire people to handle the details." Sounds good in theory, but it doesn't hold up in practice. Every business, every organization, every artistic endeavor is made up of details.

John L. McCaffrey was president of the International Harvester Company for many years. He once said, "The mechanics of running a business are not really very complicated when you get down to essentials. You have to make some stuff and sell it to somebody for more than it cost you. That's about all there is—except for a few million details."

In *The Leadership Secrets of Colin Powell*, business writer Oren Harari observed that even visionaries must be detail people. Colin Powell, he wrote, "doesn't buy into the faddish concept of the regal 'visionary' leader, the kind who stays perched on a lofty pedestal, aloof and removed, having 'delegated' all the 'trifles' of his or her so-called 'grand vision.' Good leaders know there's no solid, successful 'big picture' without the details. Both are essential—not only when the mission and strategy are being sketched out, but when they are being implemented. Effective leaders commit to both vision and detail orientation."[3]

I've racked my brain and can't think of one person of distinction and accomplishment who wasn't *both* a visionary and a detail person. In a sense, you have to have a telescope on one eye so that you can focus on your long-range vision—and a microscope on the other eye so that you can see the daily details. Your long-range vision is doomed if you ignore the little things. Harvey S. Firestone, founder of the Firestone Tire and Rubber Company, observed, "Success is the sum of details. It might perhaps be pleasing to imagine oneself beyond detail and engaged only in great things, but if one attends only to great things and lets the little things pass . . . the business shrinks."

Media mogul Rupert Murdoch operates a far-flung empire of newspapers, magazines, cable TV networks, satellite TV operations, movie studios, Internet operations, and more. Despite the vast and varied extent of his business interests, he says, "I try to keep in touch with the details. You can't keep in touch with them all, but you've got to have a feel for what's going on. I also look at the product daily.

That doesn't mean you interfere, but it's important to show the ability to be involved occasionally. It shows you understand what's happening."[4]

Admiral Hyman Rickover, the U.S. Navy's pioneering nuclear submariner, said, "I probably spend about 99 percent of my time on what others may call petty details. Most managers would rather focus on lofty policy matters, but when the details are ignored, the project fails."

Jackie Joyner-Kersee is one of the greatest women athletes of all time, having won three gold, one silver and two bronze Olympic medals. She is the first woman to score more than 7,000 points in a heptathlon event and she holds the world record in the heptathlon. The key to her success: little things. "Throughout my career," she said, "my goal was to improve 1 percent with each performance. That may sound like so little, but if I could show improvement—a tenth of a second, a few inches farther in the long jump—then I knew I was doing my best."

If all of these highly successful people think it's vital to pay attention to the little things, who are we to argue? Yes, keep the big picture in view—but never lose sight of the little things.

A Head for Details

I've heard all the excuses: "I'm not a detail person." "I don't have a head for facts." "I can't handle information overload." The truth is, we can retain any number of details if those details are important to us. You can learn to pay attention to the little things by developing a curiosity about the world. I've found that it enhances my enjoyment of my career to learn all I can about this business—in minute detail.

As a pro basketball executive, I like to wander around our facility and talk to the players, the coaches, the staffers, the interns, the concessionaires, the janitorial staff—just so that I can know how this business functions at every level. I've got the big picture, but I also know the details, because I continually ask detailed questions.

As an author, I have visited the publishing houses and talked to my editors and the production staff. I have even toured the printing facilities and have watched the massive Heidelberg presses rolling out hundreds of press sheets per second. I've seen where the printed sheets are folded, stitched, trimmed, bound and turned into books. During my tour, I talked to the workers and asked questions—lots and lots of questions.

Anyone can develop a head for details. All you have to do is develop a curiosity about the world. You'll find that the more you know, the more you *want* to know, and the more interesting life becomes. When you pay attention to the little things, the little things reward you with delight, insight and a sense of mastery and deep understanding.

The big picture is made up of details, just as many raindrops make a river and many rivers make a sea. True greatness, it has been said, comes from being great in little things. Computer visionary Max Steingart put it this way: "Good work done little by little becomes great work. Your house of success will be built brick by brick."

Or think of it this way: How can you ever achieve your vision of the future if you neglect the details of that vision? Would a painting by Rembrandt be so beautiful if the artist did not care about each brush stroke? Colin Powell said, "If you are going to achieve excellence in big things, you develop the habit in little matters. Excellence is not an exception. It is a prevailing attitude."

Would you like to be an author? Well, I can tell you from personal experience that no book exists purely as a grand vision. You must deal with thousands of details before you can hold that complete, published book in your hands. Each page, each sentence and each individual word is a "little thing" that has to be painstakingly hammered out before the book exists.

Novelist James Jones (*From Here to Eternity*) was asked, "How do you write a novel?" He replied, "It's simple. You write one page every day and at the end of the year you have 365 pages." And Zig Ziglar, in his book *Courtship After Marriage*, recalls, "I wrote *See You at the Top*, a 384-page, 2,000,000-copy bestseller, by writing an average of 1.26 pages every day for ten months."[5]

Would you like to lose weight? Do you think you can lose 30 or 40 pounds by simply having a grand vision of a thinner you? Of course not. A trim, healthy body is the result of a thousand little decisions, made with consistency and self-discipline over a period of months and years. As Zig Ziglar adds, "Seventeen years ago, I went on a diet and exercise program. I lost thirty-seven pounds in ten months by losing 1.9 ounces per day. . . . People who are successful at whatever they do reach their objectives by a series of little things they do every day."[6]

Would you like to start your own business? Then take the advice of a man who built a retail chain that has remained successful for more than a century. Charles R. Walgreen, Sr., who founded the Walgreens pharmacy chain in 1901, said, "Little extra services are the cheapest kind of advertising. It merely takes thought and a few seconds of time. Success is doing a thousand little things the right way, over and over again."

Og Mandino, in *The Spellbinder's Gift*, explains how the little things affect your career: "One of the greatest differences between a failure and a success is that the successful person will tackle chores that the failure avoids. Work done hastily, shortcuts taken, careless attention to details—these can all eventually wreak havoc on your career. Constantly remind yourself that if it is part of your work, however small a task it may be, then it is important. History still reminds us of ancient battles that were lost because of a missing horseshoe nail. *Never neglect the little things*."[7]

Would you like to be an actor? Then heed the advice of Harrison Ford, who played such roles as space pilot Han Solo and action hero Indiana Jones. As I write these words, the combined worldwide box office grosses of his films total more than $6 billion.

Ford got his start as an actor in minor TV roles on shows such as *Gunsmoke* and *Love American Style*. Not happy with the parts he was being offered, he became a carpenter to support his family and worked at various odd jobs. He built custom furniture for various Hollywood friends and constructed a sundeck for actress Sally Kellerman. Finally, director George Lucas convinced Ford to go back into acting by offering him big roles in his films *American Graffiti* and *Star Wars*. Ford's acting career soon took flight. Reflecting on what it takes to master the actor's craft, Harrison Ford says, "Acting is basically like carpentry. If you know your craft, it all comes down to details."

One February morning in 1995, I sat along with 5,000 baseball fans and current and retired players at the enshrinement ceremony at Ted Williams's Hitters Hall of Fame. The emcee of the event was broadcaster Bob Costas of NBC-TV. He stood and introduced the 30 Hall of Famers plus a number of other distinguished guests. As he introduced each one, he reeled off a list of statistics and details from each person's career. Then Bob introduced the featured speaker, former President George H. W. Bush.

During his opening remarks, Mr. Bush said, "I'd like to pay tribute to our emcee, Bob Costas. I've been sitting up here watching him introduce these great players and telling us every detail of their stellar careers. The amazing thing is that Bob didn't use one note the entire time."

Hearing that, I was amazed—but in a real sense, I wasn't surprised. Bob Costas loves baseball. I've known him for years, and I know that he has mastered every little fact about the game. When you love something that much, it's easy to pay attention to the little things.

Do a Little More, Give a Little More

Sometimes doing more than is asked and giving just a little bit more than is required can make all the difference. Kansas City businessman Mike Looney (whose son Josh was one of my interns at the Magic and now works for the Kansas City Chiefs) told me this story over lunch: "In September 1969, I was working at the weather station at a little airport in Waco,

Texas. The door opened and in walked Neil Armstrong. Just two months earlier, he had set foot on the moon. He was the most famous man in the world—but he was flying a plane from Waco to Houston. He checked in with me to get an update on weather conditions. That proved to me that, no matter how high up you go in life, you still have to pay attention to the little things."

Oscar Hammerstein II, one-half of the Rodgers and Hammerstein songwriting duo, once commented on a photo of the Statue of Liberty taken from an airplane. The picture revealed the finely sculpted strands of hair on the top of the statue's head—detail placed there by the sculptor, Frédéric-Auguste Bartholdi. The statue was dedicated in New York Harbor on October 28, 1886. At that time— almost two decades before the Wright Brothers' first flight— Bartholdi had no reason to think anyone would ever see the top of the statue. Yet the sculptor refused to cut corners. He paid attention to the little things. Hammerstein concluded, "Finish the job off perfectly. You never know when someone will fly over your work and find you out."

Jim Umbricht was a right-handed relief pitcher for the Pittsburgh Pirates (1959-1961) and the Houston Colt .45s (1962-1963). He battled cancer during his final season and died in 1964, just 33 years old.

At spring training during his rookie season in 1959, the Pirates' general manager, Branch Rickey, called a team meeting on the field. The players gathered around.

"Umbricht," Rickey said, "come up here."

Wondering what he had done wrong, Jim Umbricht stood and made his way to Branch Rickey's side.

"I saw what you did out on the field," Rickey said. "You picked up that loose ball and put it in the ball bag. That's what I like to see. You may have saved a player from stepping on that ball and spraining an ankle. Good job." Ricky took a $50 bill from his wallet and handed it to Jim Umbricht.

For the rest of his brief career, Jim Umbricht never stepped over a loose ball on the ground. He always picked it up and put it in the ball bag—not to get another $50 bill, but simply because Mr. Rickey had shown him that the little things do get noticed.

Those who devote attention to the little things eventually attract promotion and success. When you show your employers that you can manage the little things, they'll trust you with bigger things. As someone once said, "Big jobs go to those who prove they've outgrown small jobs."

Broadcaster Art Linkletter put it this way: "Do a little more than you're paid to. Give a little more than you have to. Try a little harder than you want to. Aim a little higher than you think possible." It's that little extra effort that sets you apart from your coworkers.

In his book *The Little Stuff Matters Most*, Hollywood talent manager Bernie Brillstein wrote, "Outcomes rarely turn on grand gestures, high-flying concepts, or the art of the deal—[but] more often on whether you've sent someone a thank-you note."[8]

In January 1989, the Magic organization brought comedian Bill Cosby to Orlando to perform a one-man show for the opening of our new arena. The team hadn't played one game yet, but we were rolling out our promotional merchandise, including a sweatshirt with the Magic logo.

We presented one to the Cos before he went onstage, and he wore it proudly during the show.

A decade later, in April 1999, I went with the Magic to Philly for a game against my old team, the Philadelphia 76ers. It was a rough night, and by the end of the first half, we were down 17 points. During halftime, I walked out on the floor for a stretch—and who should I see but Bill Cosby, sitting in the front row. I said, "Bill, I'm Pat Williams with the Magic!"

He jumped to his feet and pumped my hand. "Hey, man! I love my sweatshirt! I still wear it! It's my favorite!"

I was blown away. After 10 years, he remembered that Magic sweatshirt.

He grinned and added, "What's wrong with your team?"

"Bill," I said, "we didn't eat our Wheaties."

The evening ended in a 103-86 loss—our fifth loss in a row. But Bill Cosby took some of the sting out of that night by remembering one of the little things from a night 10 years earlier.

Our Lives Turn on the Little Things

George Washington Carver was born an African-American slave in 1864, in Tuskegee, Alabama. He became a painter, poet, teacher, horticulturalist, chemist and humanitarian. He invented over 100 industrial products derived from peanuts, including paints, plastics, fuels, dyes and cosmetics.

"When I was young," Carver once recalled, "I prayed, 'God, tell me the mystery of the universe.' But God answered, 'That knowledge is reserved for Me alone.' So, I said, 'Then,

God, tell me the mystery of the peanut.' And God said, 'George, that's more nearly your size.' And He told me."[9]

You and I can't know the mysteries of the universe, but we can probe the mysteries of little things. We can do little deeds of kindness. We can understand little bits of knowledge that could add up to a grand idea.

South African cleric Archbishop Desmond Tutu put it this way: "Do your little bit of good where you are. It's those little bits of good, put together, that overwhelm the world." And Oswald Chambers said, "If you want to know God's plan for your life, just do the next little thing he tells you to do."

In his autobiography, *An American Life*, Ronald Reagan, the fortieth president of the United States, reflected:

> If I'd gotten the job I wanted at Montgomery Ward, I suppose I would never have left Illinois. I've often wondered at how lives are shaped by what seem like small and inconsequential events, how an apparently random turn in the road can lead you a long way from where you intended to go—and a long way from wherever you expected to go.[10]

It's true. Our lives turn on the little things—the seemingly small events and inconsequential choices we so casually make. You could choose to go out for pizza instead of steak—and meet the person you will marry. You could choose one college over another—and meet the professor who changes the entire direction of your life. You could choose one job offer over another—and meet a mentor who unlocks the door to your dreams.

Our choices lead us to places we never expect to go. The right choices could set us on the path to unimaginable success and happiness. The wrong choices could destroy our lives. The next choice you make could trigger a chain of circumstances that could put you in the White House— or in prison. So we dare not overlook the little things.

We need to maintain our character and integrity, even in the smallest things. If we refuse to tell even a little white lie, then we'll never be convicted of perjury. If we vow never to steal even a paper clip, then we'll never be convicted of embezzlement. People who maintain their integrity in the small things can be trusted in the big things. Dr. James L. Garlow, pastor of Skyline Wesleyan Church in San Diego, put it this way:

> If you don't like who you have become, it is because of the thousands of small, seemingly insignificant decisions you have made each day over the course of the years. If you like what you have become and are becoming, it is because you have made several hundred thousand seemingly small, moment-by-moment decisions in a very wise manner. You are the sum total of your life's decisions. Most people do not realize that life is comprised of lots of little decisions—all with a huge cumulative, collective impact. Most of life is not determined by big decisions, although they are important. It is the sum total of the so-called small decisions that builds character.[11]

I'm told that Federal Express expects 100 percent accuracy from the people who sort packages. They are tested once a quarter for accuracy. Any person who fails to perform at 100 percent accuracy is sent back for retraining.

Is it expensive to maintain such high performance standards? Absolutely. But mistakes are even more expensive. Federal Express offers a premium service, and the customer pays a high price for exceptional speed and accuracy. A performance standard of 99 percent might seem good enough—unless your urgent package was part of the 1 percent that got misdirected. A 1 percent error rate would eventually cost Federal Express millions in lost customers. That's why the company demands perfection.

In the same way, you and I should demand absolute integrity of ourselves. We can't afford to settle for 99 percent integrity. We can't let ourselves off the hook by saying, "It's only a little thing." Little cracks in our integrity have a way of producing major fault lines in our character, leading to destruction.

"You can make radical changes in small steps," Zig Ziglar warns. "Remember, earthquakes and hurricanes get all the publicity, but termites do more damage than both of them combined—and the termite takes bites so small that you cannot see them with the naked eye. But they are persistent, they take lots of bites, and there are lots of termites."[12]

Donna Rice Hughes was blessed with both beauty and brains. She began modeling at age 13 and was a straight-A student throughout her high school years. An ambitious overachiever, she attended the University of South Carolina and graduated magna cum laude.

In her senior year at college, she began to compromise the faith and moral values she was raised in. She liked to party, and she stopped attending church.

In early 1987, Donna met Colorado Senator Gary Hart at a fund-raising event in Florida. The senator was on the brink of announcing his bid for the Democratic presidential nomination.

Two months later, the *National Enquirer* published a front-page photo of Donna Rice and Senator Hart on the senator's yacht, the *Monkey Business*. The 29-year-old Donna Rice was seated in 50-year-old Senator Hart's lap. A week later, Hart dropped out of the race.

Donna Rice eventually overcame the humiliation of the scandal. She married Jack Hughes in 1994, and has become an activist against pornography. The nonprofit organization she founded, "Enough Is Enough," is dedicated to making the Internet safe for children. She is also the author of *Kids Online: Protecting Your Children in Cyberspace*.

I heard Donna Rice Hughes tell her story a number of years ago at the First Baptist Church in Orlando. In spite of all the good she has done over the years, it's clear that there are significant parts of her life that she would live differently if she could. The words she spoke that day serve as a warning to us all: Neglecting the little things can have a big cost.

"I grew up in a Southern Baptist church," she said, "First Baptist Church of Columbia, South Carolina. I went to Sunday school and youth group and Sunday morning worship. I was raised to know right from wrong. But in my early twenties, I got away from my spiritual roots. I took a series of small left turns—and I ended up in an international scandal."

A series of small left turns is all it takes to destroy a reputation.

Stay on the right path, my friend, and keep on The Pursuit. Don't let those little left turns send you down a dirt road or off on some dead-end street. Pay attention to those little things. Watch them closely. Manage them well.

For good or ill, those little things will determine your destiny.

Chapter 7

The Pursuit of Wisdom

When I first arrived in Spartanburg to launch my career, I was pursuing money, glory and success. Four years later, after Mr. Littlejohn had begun to impact my life, I left Spartanburg on a totally different life Pursuit: a lifelong quest for *wisdom*.

If you have wisdom, everything you need—money, success and satisfaction in life—will come your way. But if you lack wisdom, all the money in the world can't help you.

People who have reached the pinnacle of their profession top the headlines. They have more money than anyone could spend in a natural lifetime. Millions of people recognize them. Wherever they go, the waters seem to part at their feet. Yet deep inside, they are often depressed, bored or even suicidal. They are like Marie Antoinette, the Queen of France, who in the midst of her pampered-yet-empty existence, complained, "Nothing tastes."

Wisdom is not just the key to a successful life. It's the key to enjoying your success. For those who have wisdom, life is sweet. For those who lack it, nothing tastes.

Above all else, The Pursuit is a quest for wisdom.

Wisdom: A Skill for Living

What is wisdom? Some people confuse wisdom with intelligence or learning. But as Ronald Reagan once observed, "Learning is a good thing, but unless it's tempered by faith and love of freedom, it can be very dangerous indeed. The names of many intellectuals are recorded on the rolls of infamy, from Robespierre to Lenin to Ho Chi Minh to Pol Pot." The truth is that the smartest people are sometimes unwise, and the wisest people are often unlearned.

If wisdom were a cognitive ability, you could measure it with a "wisdom quotient" test, and those with the highest WQs could join the "Wise People's Mensa." There would be wisdom college courses (Wisdom 101) and how-to books (*Wisdom for Dummies*). Kids could compete in "wisdom bees" where, instead of spelling words correctly, they would solve difficult ethical dilemmas.

But wisdom has little to do with being smart or educated. In fact, for some people, a Ph.D. degree or a genius-level IQ can interfere with genuine wisdom. Being too smart can make a fool of you. At times, the intellectual elite can be so smug about all the convolutions in their brains that they miss out on true wisdom. As mathematician Alfred North Whitehead observed, "Knowledge shrinks as wisdom grows."

In *THE MESSAGE*, pastor-author Eugene Peterson wrote, "Wisdom is not primarily knowing the truth, although it certainly includes that. It is a skill in living. For what good is a truth if we don't know how to live it? What good is an intention if we can't sustain it?"[1]

If wisdom is a skill for living, then what kind of skill is it? After years of studying and pursuing wisdom, I've concluded that it is primarily a decision-making skill. Wisdom enables us to gather information, filter it through the fine mesh of our values and principles, and make high-quality decisions that produce healthy results for ourselves and others.

Many people have the mistaken notion that wisdom comes with age. But, as newspaper columnist Leonard Pitts, Jr., has observed, "You don't get wiser because you get older. You get wiser because you work at getting wiser." I have known many young people who were wise beyond their years—and I've known a few older folk who could be described as "old fools." You can't learn wisdom unless you are teachable and eager to learn.

In a *New York Times* article, "The Older-and-Wiser Hypothesis," Stephen S. Hall tells the story of Vivian Clayton, who was probably the first researcher to make a formal academic study of wisdom. Ms. Clayton became fascinated with the subject by observing the life of her father, Simon Clayton, and her maternal grandmother, Beatrice Domb. Though her father and grandmother both had limited educations, they demonstrated serenity in times of crisis, superior decision-making ability, and a sense of contentment in times of loss or misfortune. Vivian Clayton recalled:

> My father was forty-one when I was born. . . . He had emigrated from England but had lived through World War II there and experienced the blitz and had to care for his dying mother, who was so sick that she refused to go down into the shelters

during air raids in London. She lived in the East End, where the docks were, and they were always getting bombed. So he would sit with her while the bombs were falling, and when it was over, she would say, "Now we can have a cup of tea!" He was a very humble man, and very aware of his limitations, but he always seemed to be able to weigh things and then make decisions that were right for the family.[2]

As for her maternal grandmother, Beatrice Domb, Vivian Clayton remembered her as a woman of great strength and simple contentment. Though her grandmother had less than a high school education, she was a positive role model for the entire family.

These personal observations led Ms. Clayton to explore the meaning of wisdom during her undergraduate studies in psychology at Buffalo University and later as a graduate student at the University of Southern California in the 1970s. She asked herself, *What does wisdom mean, and how does age affect it?*

She explored various fields, from gerontological research (the study of the effects of aging) to the wisdom literature of the Bible. She examined the Old Testament stories of Job and King Solomon, explored the book of Proverbs, and parsed the meanings of specific Hebrew words. She found that the ancient Hebrew word for "wisdom," *chochmah*, suggested a process of decision-making that involved both the mind and the heart, both reason and compassion.

Vivian Clayton completed her dissertation in 1976 and followed it with a number of scholarly papers. She concluded that "neither were the old always wise, nor the young lacking in wisdom." She also found that while knowledge deteriorates as people age, wisdom resists fading and its value increases as people grow older.[3]

Archie Moore (1913-1998) was a light heavyweight world boxing champion and an activist for African-American civil rights. He was also an actor who was acclaimed for his role as Jim, the runaway slave, in the film *The Adventures of Huckleberry Finn* (1960). Business writer Russell Sullivan once told a story from Archie Moore's boxing days:

Moore . . . cast himself as a homespun philosopher. In training camp, he would occasionally meditate while reading the New Testament. And he was constantly regaling the press with bits of wisdom, often in the form of proverbs and platitudes.

"You're no philosopher," Moore once said to a training camp observer. "You're too young to be a philosopher."

The man replied, "I'm forty-one. I'm older than you, yet you claim to be a philosopher."

Answered Moore, "You're older perhaps, but you gotta suffer to be a philosopher. I've suffered, so I'm a philosopher."[4]

Archie Moore makes a good point: Suffering can produce wisdom. As novelist Pearl S. Buck observed, "There is an alchemy in sorrow. It can be transmuted into wisdom."

Wisdom for Your Career and Financial Life

Permit me to share a few of the wise insights I've collected over the years from Mr. Littlejohn and other mentors, as well as from my own experience. First, here are some nuggets of practical wisdom to help you manage your career and financial security:

- *Money can't buy happiness.* When choosing a career, don't decide on the basis of money alone. Do what you love and the money will come.

- *Earn your keep.* Your boss doesn't owe you a job. You have to earn it every day. Everybody wants a raise. What have you done to earn yours?

- *Don't be a clock-watcher.* Come in early. Leave late. Give more than you have to. Increase your employer's profits so that he or she can afford to give you that raise.

- *Be kind to everyone.* Be nice to people above you and below you—and even to people you don't like. It doesn't cost you anything, and someday it may pay dividends.

- *Focus on the good.* Share the credit for every achievement. Be stingy with criticism; be lavish with praise. When you make others look good, you look good.

- *It's wise to be humble.* You're not too important to pick up papers, arrange chairs or make coffee.

- *Embrace change.* Don't get set in a one-size-fits-all mentality.

- *Seek out wise counsel.* Be more eager to receive constructive criticism than praise. A compliment feels good, but nobody ever learned anything new from a pat on the back.

- *When you've nothing to say, say nothing.* Ben Franklin observed, "Silence is not always a sign of wisdom, but babbling is ever a sign of folly."

- *Never bluff.* If you don't know the answer, say, "I don't know—but I'll find out."

- *Whatever happens, don't panic.* Think it through. Every problem has a solution. Well, almost every problem.

- *When you mess up, 'fess up.* If your boss corrects you, take it graciously and learn from it. Don't be defensive. Don't argue.

- *Stay out of the muck.* Stay clear of office politics, backstabbing and manipulation. Never betray a confidence. Mind your own business.

- *Don't misjudge your superiors.* Your boss is not as stupid as you think. Don't underestimate him or her. Whatever you're hiding, your boss probably knows—or soon will.

- *Live within your means.* You can't borrow your way to prosperity. You can't spend your way to riches. Financial security is the result of hard work, disciplined spending and prudent investing.

- *Take risks.* When presented with two equal options, choose the bolder of the two. Don't take foolish chances, but don't be afraid to take calculated risk. The greater the risk, the greater the potential reward.

- *Be positive.* "Perpetual optimism is a force multiplier," said Colin Powell. With an optimistic attitude, you can go farther, endure longer and achieve more than you ever imagined.

- *Be decisive.* This doesn't mean you should make snap decisions. But once the choice becomes clear, make your decision firmly and take responsibility for it. Instead of wondering if you made the right decision, do everything you can to make it come out right.

- *Base your decisions on values and principles.* Roy Disney (Walt's brother and business partner) said, "When your values are clear, making decisions becomes easier."

One reason Mr. Littlejohn made such confident, high-quality decisions was that he knew his values. His decisions were dictated by his principles. I don't recall ever seeing Mr.

Littlejohn agonizing over a decision. He came to a conclusion, made a decision and implemented it.

And he was almost never wrong.

Wisdom for Everyday Life

Next, permit me to share some concise but life-transforming nuggets of insight for your everyday life:

- *Pursue wisdom, not money.* An old proverb says, "The wise know the value of riches, but the rich do not know the pleasures of wisdom."

- *Strive for personal growth.* You'll know you're becoming wise when your actions are motivated by self-discipline instead of external rewards and punishments. The Greek playwright Aristophanes said, "A wise man would live the same life even if all the laws were abolished."

- *Don't procrastinate.* As Charles H. Spurgeon said, " 'Now' is the watchword of the wise." Don't put off personal goals until that far-off day "when I have more time." Every day is 24 hours long, and you'll never get a 25-hour day.

- *Never give in to envy.* Most of the unhappiness we suffer comes from comparing ourselves to others. Be satisfied with who you are and what you have. The richest people of all are those who are content with what they have.

- *Guard your integrity.* There's no excuse for even a little dishonesty. It takes years to build trust and only seconds to destroy it. Wear your moral compass like a wristwatch, and consult it regularly.

- *Never receive or spread gossip.* Be as careful with the reputations of others as you'd have them be with yours. If you must talk about other people, make sure it's good news, not bad.

- *Keep an open mind.* As you mature, continually revise your opinions. Be open to new information, new insights and new ways of perceiving the world. Novelist Robert Louis Stevenson said, "To hold the same views at forty that we held at twenty is to have been stupefied for a score of years."

- *Take care of yourself.* Eat right, exercise and get regular checkups. No amount of wealth can help you if you lose your health.

- *Seek wisdom from God.*

King Solomon reigned over Israel from about 970 to 928 B.C. According to rabbinical tradition, he was 12 years old when he ascended the throne, and he grew to be the wisest man who ever lived. In 1 Kings 3, we see that Solomon made only one request of God. He didn't ask for riches, long life or victory over his enemies. He asked only for wisdom: "a discerning heart to govern your people and to distinguish between right and wrong" (1 Kings 3:9). God honored Solomon's request.

Wisdom ultimately comes from God. Elsewhere we read, "If any of you lacks wisdom, he should ask God, who gives generously to all without finding fault, and it will be given to him" (Jas. 1:5).

When my son Bobby became a manager in the Washington Nationals farm system at the age of 27, I told him, "If you ever need wisdom in a hurry, all you have to do is say to God, 'Lord, I need wisdom quick! What should I do?' And the wisdom you need will be there. He has promised to give it to you."

That's a promise for you to take and test for yourself. Ask God for wisdom—and the moment you ask, your answer will be on its way.

Chapter 8

The Mindset of a Learner

In mid-1997, I flew to Detroit to speak to executives of the Ford Motor Company. The limo that was to pick me up at the airport never arrived, so after an hour, I arranged another ride. I got to the hotel, where a newly hired desk clerk was being trained on the job. There was a customer ahead of me, and the entire process was painfully slow.

It was late, I was exhausted and my patience was frayed. I paced, I muttered, I blew steam out of my ears, and I sighed those deep Al Gore sighs. Of course, none of my fussing and fuming helped one bit.

Finally, the clerk finished registering the customer in front of me. It was my turn—but just as I stepped up to the desk, the clerk said, "One moment, sir—I'll be right back."

I moaned and rolled my eyes.

The customer who had registered ahead of me turned. "Sir," he said, "the clerk is new on the job and he's nervous, but he's really doing the best he can. You could try to be a little more understanding."

Well, I instantly felt two inches tall. The man was right. I felt foolish and embarrassed—and I wondered if that man was going to be in the audience for my speech.

The clerk returned and checked me in—and I took great pains to be gracious.

The next morning, as I came out of my room and headed for the elevator, there he was—the customer who had gently lectured me the previous night. "We meet again," he said pleasantly.

"I'm glad," I said. "I'm sorry for my behavior last night. You're right—I was rude. Thanks for having the courage to speak up." We had a nice chat in the elevator.

As it turned out, he wasn't with Ford, so he wouldn't be at my speech. What a relief! We reached the lobby and went our separate ways.

I had come to Dearborn to lecture—and I had received a lesson instead. It was a lesson in being patient, kind and understanding, even when I'm feeling tired, cranky and not at my best.

It was, above all, a lesson in wisdom.

Curious About Everything

If you want to grow in wisdom, there are five things you must do on a continual basis: (1) learn, (2) question, (3) listen, (4) read, and (5) acquire mentors. First, let's explore what it means to be a lifelong learner.

1. Continually Learn

Author Benjamin Barber once observed, "I divide the world into learners and non-learners. There are people who learn, who are open to what happens around them, who listen, who hear the lessons. When they do something stupid, they don't do it again. And when they do something that works a little bit, they do it even better and harder the next time. The question to ask is not whether you are a success or a failure, but whether you are a learner or a non-learner."[1]

To have the mindset of a learner, you must cultivate the art of curiosity. Eleanor Roosevelt, who was a much-beloved and influential American first lady from 1933 to 1945, was educated at a girls' boarding school in Allenswood, England. The school was run by the French feminist educator Marie Souvestre, whose mission in life was to teach young women to be independent thinkers. When young Eleanor came to Mlle. Souvestre's school, she was an avid learner, even though she had been taught by her mother that curiosity was a character flaw (as in the adage, "Curiosity killed the cat").

One evening, Eleanor and the other girls were gathered in the library of the school. Mlle. Souvestre showed them the room filled with books and hidden knowledge, and said, "Many of you have been taught that curiosity is a fault. Rubbish! Ladies, you must cultivate the art of curiosity! Only by being curious and inquisitive will you learn the wonders contained in these books—and the wonders all around you in the world of people and ideas."

At that moment, young Eleanor felt that her mind was finally set free to fly wherever it wanted. The gift of unbridled curiosity was finally hers to enjoy. Decades later, she said, "One thing life has taught me: If you are interested in the world, you never have to look for new interests. They come to you. When you are genuinely interested in one thing, it will always lead to something else."

We should learn from all kinds of people—not only those who are older and wiser than we are, but from people we might tend to overlook. Bill Cosby put it this way: "No matter where you work, seek out the janitor. They know everything and they know everybody. Don't ever think you know more than someone who's mopping a floor."

I hired Chuck Daly to his first NBA coaching job with the Philadelphia 76ers in 1977. Soon after he joined the 76ers organization, he learned that it is important, when drawing up your game plan, to consult with your players. Chuck told me, "Julius Erving came to me shortly after I came aboard. He said, 'Do you know where every player on this team wants a shot from?' You see, a lot of coaches have a play designed and they don't take into consideration whether or not a player likes to take a shot from that spot. Ever since Julius asked me that question, I have made a point of asking each player where he feels most comfortable shooting from. I try to get him a shot from that spot. Julius taught me that."

Whenever I go to another city for a speaking engagement, I enjoy talking to the limousine driver who takes me from place to place. One driver I met, Don Lynch, has been driving authors in Chicago for years. I asked Don which authors he remembered best, and he named Amy Tan, Dave Barry, Suzanne Somers, Lucy Arnaz, Richard Bach and several others.

I said, "Is there one positive trait they all have in common?"

"Absolutely," he said. "They all ask questions. They are curious about everything."

Ralph Waldo Emerson once observed, "Every man I meet is my master in some point and in that I learn from him." It's true. We can all learn something from just about anyone. This point was vividly brought home to me in a story I once read in *Guideposts*, written by a nurse named Joanne C. Jones.

During her second year of nursing school, one of Ms. Jones's professors surprised the class with a pop quiz. The test seemed easy, and Ms. Jones breezed through all the questions—until she reached the last one. The question read, "What is the first name of the cleaning lady at this school?"

Ms. Jones wondered if the question was a joke. She had seen the cleaning lady in the halls, going about her work—but what was her name? She had to leave the question blank.

After the exam, Ms. Jones asked, "Does the last question count toward our grade?"

"It certainly does," replied the professor. "In your nursing career, every person you meet is significant and deserves to be greeted by name."

Ms. Jones concluded, "I've never forgotten the lesson I learned that day. I also learned that the woman's name was Dorothy."

2. Continually Question

In *We Shall Not Fail: The Inspiring Leadership of Winston Churchill*, the granddaughter of Winston Churchill, Celia Sandys, wrote, "To know the right questions to ask, you need some basic knowledge. By reading voraciously, Winston Churchill knew the history of warfare and weapons through the ages, as well as the latest fantasies from science fiction writers such as H. G. Wells. Churchill's advantage was that he never feared asking what others might think was a stupid or naïve question."[2]

What should we question? Everything! Questions lead us down new paths of discovery. Bernard Baruch, advisor to Presidents Wilson and Roosevelt, said, "Millions saw the apple fall, but Isaac Newton asked why." To be a life-long learner, ask questions. Find people who know more than you do and ask away! You won't be imposing. They'll be gratified that someone is eager to hear what they have to say.

When you talk to friends, family, professors and people on the street, hone your skill as an interviewer. Spend at least 80 percent of your conversation asking questions. Learn to hold back your own opinions while soaking up knowledge and ideas from others.

I host three different talk radio shows every week in Orlando, and I certainly don't get wealthy doing them. So why do I do them? It's because I'm constantly trying to improve my interviewing skills. I try to get as much insight and information from my guests as I can in a 30-minute period. My mission is to ask as many one-sentence questions as I can, and I always follow the advice of Rudyard Kipling. In *Just So Stories for Little Children*, he wrote:

> I keep six honest serving-men
> (They taught me all I knew);
> Their names are What and Why and When
> And How and Where and Who.

So whether you are in front of a microphone or in a one-on-one conversation, ask one-sentence questions beginning with one of Kipling's "six honest serving-men," and you'll be amazed at what you learn.

Practice asking open-ended questions that don't have yes or no answers. When you ask a question, listen carefully before going on to the next question. Be patient. Don't interrupt. Don't be too quick to fill in the pauses with talk. Give the other person time to think. If you ask too many rapid-fire questions, you choke off thought and the other person feels rushed. To get thoughtful answers, ask thoughtful questions.

Above all, seek out people who have lived longer and achieved more than you. Ask them the secrets of their wisdom and success. As the old proverb says, "To know the road ahead, ask those who are coming back."

3. Continually Listen

Someone once noted that God gave us two ears but only one mouth. The reason: He wants us to listen twice as much as we talk. CNN interviewer Larry King has built a career on being a good listener. He once said, "I remind myself every morning that nothing I say this day will teach me anything. So, if I'm going to learn, I must do it by listening." And author Frank Tyger once said, "Be a good listener. Your ears never get you in trouble."

Listening is a skill. Self-help author and speaker Brian Tracy talked about the skill of listening on his blog:

The wonderful thing is, when you practice effective listening, other people will begin to find you fascinating. They will want to be around you. They will feel relaxed and happy in your presence. . . . Listening builds trust. The more you listen to another person, the more he or she trusts you and believes in you.

Listening also builds self-esteem. When you listen attentively to another person, his or her self-esteem will naturally increase.

Finally, listening builds self-discipline in the listener. Because your mind can process words at 500-600 words per minute, and we can only talk at about 150 words per minute, it takes a real effort to keep your attention focused on another person's words. If you do not practice self-discipline in conversation, your mind will wander in a hundred different directions. The more you work at paying close attention to what the other person is saying, the more self-disciplined you will become. In other words, by learning to listen well, you actually develop your own character and your own personality.[3]

Many people think of a listener as the person in the passive role of a conversation. But effective listening is far from passive. To truly listen takes focused concentration. It's a tiring activity. A good listener is constantly thinking, processing and giving the talker nonverbal cues (eye contact, a nod, a smile). You can only listen to somebody for so long before you need to take a break. Active listening is hard work.

In April 2007, I was shocked and saddened to hear that David Halberstam, author of *The Best and the Brightest*, was killed in a traffic accident in Menlo Park, near San Francisco.

I had interviewed David many times on my radio show, and it was hard to believe that a man who had survived a harrowing stint as a reporter in the Vietnam War would come to his end as a victim of a random traffic accident.

Anna Quindlen wrote a tribute to her longtime friend David Halberstam, saying, "He was the most curious person I have ever known. His totem was the question mark. Sometimes he would turn himself into one, head lowered, broad back curved. . . . He was an aerobic listener." I love that description! Halberstam truly was an aerobic listener—someone who put his whole body into the act of listening. He was a role model of what it means to be an active listener.[4]

When listening, use your eyes as well as your ears. We tend to think that communication is only about words. In reality, much (if not most) of communication is nonverbal. Factors like body language, tone of voice, facial expression and eye contact have a profound effect on our everyday communication. We need to listen with our eyes in order to understand what people are really saying to us.

Let's say you're talking with a coworker at the office. She says, "The boss's speech was absolutely brilliant!" There's no mistaking those words, is there? Well, let's think about it.

Suppose she said those words in a derisive tone of voice, with her arms crossed in front of her while she rolled her eyes disdainfully. Now we know that her statement was meant sarcastically. All the visual, nonverbal cues she added to her message actually inverted the meaning of her words. What she literally said was completely the opposite of what she meant. So always listen with your eyes as well as your ears.

Resist the temptation to interrupt, change the subject or top the other person's story with one of your own. If someone says, "Let me finish," take it as a sign that you interrupt too freely. Cutting people off to make your point does not make you more persuasive; it only makes you more abrasive. If you want to win people to your point of view, listen more and interrupt less.

Listening is a great way to win friends and influence people. Dale Carnegie, one of the first and best-known self-help authors, recalled a dinner party he attended, hosted by a New York publisher. There, Carnegie became acquainted with a botanist. Having never had a conversation with a botanist before, Carnegie took the man aside and spent the entire evening questioning the man about plants and gardens. By the time the evening ended, Carnegie was embarrassed to realize that he had ignored the other guests while talking to the botanist for hours.

The next morning, Carnegie called the host of the party and apologized for monopolizing the botanist for the entire evening. "I'm afraid that was rude of me," he said.

The publisher replied, "Nonsense! Your botanist friend was quite impressed with you. In fact, he told me you are the most interesting conversationalist he's ever met."

Carnegie was astonished. The botanist had done all the talking. Carnegie had merely listened. But then he realized that giving another human being the gift of complete attention offers one of the greatest compliments you can ever pay someone.

Dale Carnegie later said, "The secret of influencing people lies not so much in being a good talker as in being a good listener. Ask questions. Encourage others to express their ideas fully. They will never forget, and you will learn a thing or two."

Listening is a valuable job skill. Norm Augustine, former CEO of Martin Marietta, observed, "One often hears the remark, 'He talks too much.' But when was the last time you heard anyone say, 'He listens too much'?" Calvin Coolidge once said, "No one ever listened himself out of a job." And it's worth noting that "silent" is an anagram for "listen"—just rearrange the letters and there's a message there. So practice your listening skills and advance in your career.

The late humorist and publisher Bennett Cerf told the story of a university professor who would invite students to his home for informal dinners. At one dinner party, a student asked, "Professor, tell us the secret of being a good conversationalist."

The professor raised one finger and said, "Listen."

All around the table, the students leaned forward and waited for the professor's next words. A long, uncomfortable silence passed.

Finally, a student said, "We're listening."

The professor smiled and said, "That's the secret."

4. Continually Read

To gain wisdom, become a voracious reader. According to Brian Tracy, the highest-earning 10 percent of Americans read two to three hours a day. They read books, newspapers and magazines to expand their knowledge base and stay current. Contrast these high-achieving Americans with the average adult. Tracy reports that, according to the American Booksellers Association, 80 percent of American households have not purchased or read one book in the past year. Conclusion? The average American doesn't read at all—and that's probably why he's so average!

I'll never understand why people avoid the pleasure of reading. Go to any doctor's office, the Department of Motor Vehicles or an airport lounge—anyplace where people sit and wait. How many do you see reading a book? Usually none. I'm on commercial flights all the time, and as I walk down the aisle of a big jumbo jet, I often check to see what (if anything) people are reading. If I spot just two book readers on the entire plane, it's a lot. Most passengers are fiddling with computers or watching a movie—but no books. For some unfathomable reason, most people would rather sit and stare at their fingernails than read a good book.

Reading is easy, fun and rewarding. Any reasonably intelligent person can read a book a week. That adds up to 52 books a year, or 520 books over the next decade. With just a small amount of effort each day, you can vastly expand your mind. Make reading a daily habit; the wisdom you acquire could make you one of the most successful people in your field. As Brian Tracy observes, "The more ideas you expose yourself to, the more likely it is that you will expose yourself to the right idea at the right time."

The benefits of reading are innumerable. Even if you never finished college, you can become a well-rounded, well-educated person through reading. The books you read will increase your vocabulary, make you a more interesting person, teach you to think clearly and logically, and give you a deeper understanding of the world you live in. Here are eight tips for becoming a more effective reader.

1. *Plan and schedule regular time for reading.* If you can't set aside an hour or two, make it 15 minutes a day—but read every day without fail.

2. *Read broadly.* Avoid reading only in your favorite subjects or your favorite field. Go outside your normal range of interests and let reading make you a deeper, broader person. (For more insights into how reading can transform your life, see *Read for Your Life* by Pat Williams with Peggy Matthews Rose.)

   Pastor Mark Evans of the Church at Rock Creek in Little Rock, Arkansas, once talked about his eclectic reading habits. "I'm not an atheist," he said, "but I've read the writings of Bertrand Russell, one of the most famous atheists of the twentieth century. Why? Because when I read things that are outside the normal routine of my life, it challenges me and expands my horizons. In the process of doing so, I find that I am using parts of my mind that would otherwise stay dormant."

3. *Be a choosy reader.* Close to a thousand new titles are published every day—and many are simply not worth reading. Select books that will improve your mind and increase your wisdom and

knowledge. Historian James Bryce said, "Life is too short to spend it reading inferior books."

4. *Take books with you wherever you go.* Anytime you are going to have "time to kill," don't kill it—fill it with a good book. Business writer Tom Peters says, "My pre-travel ritual is that it takes me 10 minutes to pack my clothes and somewhere between several hours and several days to choose the books I'll take along."

5. *Don't rush.* Read at your own pace. Speed comes with practice. Beware of speed-reading techniques that limit retention of what you've read. As comedian Woody Allen once said, "I took a speed-reading course where you run your finger down the middle of the page and I was able to read *War and Peace* in 20 minutes. It's about Russia."

6. *Don't just read a book; interact with it.* Mark up your books. Highlight passages that resonate with your thinking—and those passages that challenge your opinions. Argue with the author and write ideas and questions in the margin. Writer Elbert Hubbard said, "I do not read a book. I hold a conversation with the author."

7. *Build your own library.* Every home should be well furnished with books. In 1933, Yale professor

William Lyon Phelps gave a radio talk about his
6,000-volume personal library:

We enjoy reading books that belong to us much
more than if they are borrowed. A borrowed
book is like a guest in the house. . . . You must
see that it sustains no damage; it must not suffer while under your roof. You cannot leave it
carelessly, you cannot mark it, you cannot turn
down the pages, you cannot use it familiarly.
And then, some day, although this is seldom
done, you really ought to return it.

But your own books belong to you; you treat
them with that affectionate intimacy that anni-
hilates formality. Books are for use, not for show;
you should own no book that you are afraid to
mark up, or afraid to place on the table, wide
open and face down. . . .

Everyone should begin collecting a private
library in youth. . . . One should have one's
own bookshelves, which should not have
doors, glass windows, or keys; they should be
free and accessible to the hand as well as to the
eye. . . . Most of my indoor life is spent in a
room containing six thousand books; and I
have a stock answer to the invariable question
that comes from strangers. "Have you read all
of these books?"

"Some of them twice." This reply is both
true and unexpected.[5]

8. *Finally, share your reading experience with others.*
   Join book discussion clubs, in which like-minded
   book lovers read and talk about good books.
   Recommend your favorite books to friends, and
   then exchange and discuss insights with them.
   Exploring books with other people deepens your
   understanding and increases the wisdom you
   gain from a good book.

Antiquarian bookseller Nathan Pine once observed,
"There's something special about people who are interested
in the printed word. They are a species all their own—learned,
kind, knowledgeable, and human." And artist Michelle Oka
Doner recalled, "Our accountant nearly dropped dead when
he saw what I spent on books last year. My husband said, 'I
guess he doesn't know too many people who would spend
more money on books than on clothes.'"

Through books we peer into great minds, discover great
thoughts and absorb the wisdom of the ages. Publisher
Charles Scribner II said, "Reading is a means of thinking
with another person's mind. It forces you to stretch your
own." And Canadian novelist and playwright Robertson
Davies observed, "A truly great book should be read in
youth, again in maturity, and once more in old age, as a
fine building should be seen by morning light, at noon,
and by midnight."

If the wisdom of the ages is found in books, then the
most surpassing wisdom of all is found in the Bible. One
person you'll meet in its pages is the apostle Paul. He wrote
many letters that are contained in the New Testament. At

the end of one letter, written from Mamertine Prison in Rome, Paul said, "Bring the cloak that I left with Carpus at Troas when you come—and the books, especially the parchments" (2 Tim. 4:13, *NKJV*). In books we find not only knowledge and wisdom, but comfort for the soul.

Learn Wisdom from Mentors

If you would be wise, be mentored. As C. S. Lewis said, "The wisest man is the one with the largest circle of counselors." And Woodrow Wilson said, "I use not only all the brains I have but all I can borrow." I am the product of my mentors. I have had literally dozens of mentors who have generously shared their wisdom with me. Without their investment in my life, I would not be where I am today.

Foremost of all my mentors was Mr. R. E. Littlejohn. I could not have received a more intensive education than the "doctorate" I received from Littlejohn University. Mr. R. E. was the most extraordinary man I've ever known, and from the day I met him, I wanted to pattern my life after his. Down through the years, whenever I've faced a difficult ethical decision, my first question was always, "What would Mr. Littlejohn do?"

Mr. Littlejohn was older and wiser—but I have also had mentors who were younger. One of my closest friends and mentors today is Jay Strack, founder of Student Leadership University. He counsels me, encourages me and sometimes confronts me. He makes me feel affirmed and valued. He even laughs at my jokes—which is not easy to do!

How can you find a mentor who will guide you and give you the same advantages I've been so blessed to have? Here are 10 suggestions:

1. *Seek out good role models.* Who are the successful, accomplished people who are living out the same dreams you're pursuing? The ideal mentor shares your values and worldview but may have a personality and skills that are different from your own. Those differences can help you learn new ways of thinking and solving problems.

2. *Approach the prospective mentor with care.* Don't say, "Please be my mentor." Successful, high-achieving people are busy—and the word "mentor" can sound time-consuming and could scare off a possible mentor. Instead, approach that person and ask for insight regarding one specific issue or problem. Then see how the relationship develops from there.

3. *Respect the prospective mentor's time.* Avoid taking up more than 10 to 15 minutes. Ask a limited number of questions, and take notes. Show this person that you are a serious learner.

4. *Learn to accept criticism from your mentor.* A mentor is not a cheerleader. A mentor is a coach—and coaches sometimes have to be tough on you. Don't be defensive or argumentative. Learn the

lesson your mentor is trying to teach you, and one day you'll appreciate the lesson.

5. *Take full responsibility for your own life.* You want a mentor, not a babysitter. Don't ask the mentor to make decisions for you, meet your emotional needs or take charge of your life. You want insight and wisdom so that you can make your own decisions.

6. *Take it slowly.* See if there is chemistry between you and your mentor. Allow a relationship to unfold naturally.

7. *Be polite and gracious.* Send thank-you notes, expressing gratitude for your mentor's investment of time and insight. Check in from time to time and share your triumphs, career developments and good news.

8. *Be supportive.* Find ways to repay your mentor's kindness. Attend public events where your mentor is featured or honored (a speaking engagement, a concert or an award ceremony). Show your appreciation.

9. *Feel free to have more than one mentor at a time.* And continue to pursue mentoring relationships throughout your career. You are never too old to learn new lessons in wisdom.

10. *Pay it forward.* You can never pay your mentor back for his or her investment in your life, but you can always pay it forward by becoming a mentor to others.

Be a Sponge for Wisdom

As a father to 19 children, all of them grown, I've made a fascinating observation: The ones who seek wisdom from others (parents, coaches, teachers, mentors) have become successful at an early age and are making great strides in pursuing their goals.

But those who go their own way, make their own mistakes and reject counsel and wisdom from others—well, they've struggled. They're great young people with good hearts, and I love them all—but life is harder for them and they are not achieving their goals. A few don't seem to have goals.

Sometimes my kids will tell me, "I saw Tim Russert at the mall" or "I saw Amy Grant downtown." I'll say, "Did you talk to him?" or "What did she say?" And they'll reply, "I didn't want to intrude."

I'm always amazed by that answer! When I see famous people, I *always* talk to them. I want some of their success and wisdom to rub off on me and become a part of my life. Even if there's only enough time for a handshake, I want that handshake! If there's time for a couple of questions, all the better: "Who had the greatest influence and impact on your life? What was that person's greatest strength or trait?" I've asked questions of great people for years, and by asking those few simple questions, I've accumulated a vast treasure trove of wise insights.

In June 2005, I was invited to the twenty-fifth anniversary celebration of the Washington Speakers Bureau. The guest list was stellar: Lou Holtz, Madeleine Albright, Rudy Giuliani, Joe Theismann, and more. At the reception, I was at the dessert table—and there, right in arm's reach of me, was Colin Powell. He was grabbing an éclair before heading out the door.

"General Powell," I said, "I'm Pat Williams of the Orlando Magic. My son Bobby has just become a manager in the Washington Nationals farm system. Would you have any advice for him?"

Powell said, "Tell your son, 'Take care of the troops.'" He paused. "And tell him, 'Keep your mouth shut and do your job.'" He started to leave, then stopped one final time and said over his shoulder, "And, 'Don't worry about your next job.'" Then he was out the door.

I quickly grabbed a cocktail napkin and wrote down the three pieces of advice General Powell had given me. It was a short course in wise leadership, delivered in 20 seconds.

Whenever you encounter wise, successful people, don't be afraid to ask questions. You aren't bothering them or imposing on them. In fact, you compliment them when you ask for their advice—and they love to dispense it. Always be a sponge for wisdom.

The Results of Wisdom

After spending time with Mr. Littlejohn, I always came away feeling transformed in two important ways: First, I felt *con-*

fident to face my problems and make good decisions. Second, I felt *empowered* to handle any situation. Let's take a closer look at confidence and empowerment, the two results of wisdom:

1. Confidence

After reading Jon Krakauer's book *Into Thin Air*, the account of the loss of eight climbers on Mount Everest, I became obsessed with the idea of climbing a mountain. I had never done it before and I wondered if I could. I'm so scared of heights that, when I was a boy, my tree house was built on a stump. But I was ready for a challenge—and you can't call anything a challenge if it doesn't scare you.

I arranged to join a group of amateur climbers on Mount Rainier, a semi-dormant volcano in the Cascade Range of west-central Washington State. Topping out at 14,410 feet, it's the tallest glaciated peak in the 48 contiguous states, and is often used as a practice slope for climbers who are preparing an assault on Everest. I bought my climbing equipment and arrived at the foot of the mountain in September 1996.

Our guide was an elite climber named George Dunn— a ruggedly built man of 6'3" who had climbed Everest and stood at the top of the world. I placed my life in George Dunn's experienced hands, and I followed him around like a puppy dog. The man exuded confidence.

After we began our climb, an unseasonable whiteout blizzard accompanied by high winds and deep snowdrifts slowed our progress. I had never experienced such conditions before, and my confidence wavered. I said, "George, have you ever seen anything like this?"

He grinned. "This is like a good day on Mount Everest," he said.

I felt a lot better hearing that. If George Dunn's confidence was unshaken, then I knew I'd be okay. As it turned out, we didn't make it to the summit. The blizzard forced my group to turn back when I was 3,000 feet shy of the summit. But I learned a lot about confidence from my encounter with the mountain.

Confidence is the key to The Pursuit of your goals. With confidence, you can reach astounding heights. Without it, you'll never get off the ground.

Yankees slugger Babe Ruth once promised a sick boy that he would hit a ball out of the park for him—and he did. As Ruth left the ballpark after the game, a reporter asked, "What if you had struck out?" The Babe blinked in surprise. "I never thought of that," he said. That's confidence.

Babe Didrikson Zaharias was one of the greatest woman athletes of all time. As a girl, she was nicknamed after Babe Ruth when she hit five home runs in a baseball game. As a young woman, she achieved stellar success in a variety of sports, from track and field to basketball to golf. She was also an expert diver, bowler and roller skater. She was even a singer and harmonica player who recorded several hit songs on the Mercury Records label in the 1930s.

At the 1932 Olympic Games in Los Angeles, she won three medals—two gold and a silver—for track and field. She would have won more, but the rules limited her to three events. She later went on to become a dominant golfer of the 1940s and 1950s. The *New York Times* said of her, "Except perhaps for Arnold Palmer, no golfer has ever been more beloved by the gallery." She was diagnosed with colon cancer in 1953. She made a comeback after her surgery, but her cancer returned in 1955, limiting her schedule. Battling bravely to the end, she succumbed to the cancer in 1956, at the age of 45.

Babe Zaharias packed more accomplishments into her brief life than most other people even dare dream of. Her pursuit of life was intense and exciting, though it was all too short. The reason she accomplished so much: confidence.

On one occasion, at the beginning of a golf match, she arrived at the first tee and announced, "The Babe is here. Who's coming in second?" She once told an interviewer, "It's not enough just to swing at the ball. You've got to loosen your girdle and really let the ball have it."[6] That's how she approached golf—and life.

When you have confidence, you hear that quiet voice within you that says, "I am becoming what I am capable of being." Once you have confidence, everything is possible.

2. Empowerment

Empowerment is more than just a pat on the back and a pep talk. To be genuinely empowered is to know that you are doing meaningful, important work, that you are contributing to the lives of others, and that you are following God's plan for your life.

In the Bible, we see that Jesus mentored the 12 disciples and empowered them to dare great things. He told them, "Anyone who has faith in me will do what I have been doing. He will do even greater things than these" (John 14:12). Albert Schweitzer (1875- 1965), the Nobel-winning philosopher and physician, once said, "In everyone's life at some time, the inner fire goes out. It is then burst into flame by an encounter with another human being. We should all be grateful for those people who rekindle our inner spirit." That's the kind of empowerment our mentors instill in us at key moments of our lives.

John Maxwell tells a story about Coach Vince Lombardi of the Green Bay Packers. One day during practice, an offensive linemen kept missing his blocking assignments and letting the defenders get through. So Lombardi bawled the player out, leaving him dejected and nearly destroyed.

After practice, Lombardi passed through the locker room and saw his victim sitting on a bench, head down, almost in tears. The coach walked over, mussed the player's hair, slapped him on the shoulder and said, "Don't let it get you down, Jerry. I believe in you. One of these days, you're gonna be the best offensive lineman in the NFL."

That player was Jerry Kramer. True to Lombardi's words, Kramer went on to become a dominant offensive player, a member of the Green Bay Packers Hall of Fame and the NFL's All Fifty-Year Team. Jerry Kramer points to that moment as the turning point in his career. "Coach Lombardi's encouragement impacted my whole life. When I was at my lowest point, he told me I was going to be the best, and I carried that image of myself for the rest of my career." Vince Lombardi was a tough coach—and a great empowerer.

As poet Maya Angelou once said, "People will forget what you said. People will forget what you did. But people will never forget how you made them feel." Empowerment is like oxygen to the soul. We need a steady supply in order to keep moving forward in The Pursuit.

God created us to do great things. We will fulfill our purpose if we are confident and empowered, and if we expect great things of ourselves.

Be Aware of Your Influence

Once wisdom has produced confidence and empowerment in your life, you will possess a quality called *influence*.

I spoke to a Rotary Club meeting in Windermere, Florida. A man named George Bailey introduced me, and after my talk, George and I chatted. He told me he'd read my autobiography, *Ahead of the Game*, and said, "You've been very fortunate to have so many mentors in your life."

"Yes," I said, "I've been very blessed by my mentors."

"And now you're one of them," George said.

That was a sobering and humbling thought. We are all responsible for our influence on others. Henrietta Mears, the woman who mentored such leaders as the late Senate chaplain Richard C. Halverson and Dr. Billy Graham, said, "Your influence is either negative or it's positive. Your influence is never neutral."

Pat Jordan is a former minor league pitcher and a sportswriter with *The Sporting News*. He recalled a boyhood encounter with one of his heroes, Hall of Fame shortstop Phil Rizzuto, at a Yankees game. "I was nine years old, and when the game was over, I rushed down to the dugout and hung over with a scrap of paper and beseeched Phil Rizzuto to sign it. He did, gave it back, and smiled. I lost the paper, but I still have the smile."[7] Now *that's* influence.

People are much more deeply impacted by your example than by anything you say. So act as if the whole world is watching—because it is.

Ultimately, The Pursuit is all about the life you are building, the influence you are having on others and the legacy you are leaving behind. Don't waste this present moment, my friend. Don't make the mistake of thinking that your life goes on forever. It doesn't. Tomorrow is uncertain; the day after tomorrow even more so.

If you're going to accomplish anything worthwhile in this life, if you are going to have an influence and leave a legacy, you must start now. As human rights activist Walter E. Fauntroy told the graduating class at Howard University:

> The past is yours. Learn from it. The future is yours. Fulfill it. Knowledge is yours. Use it. Cancer is yours. Cure it. Racism is yours. End it. Injustice is yours. Correct it. Sickness is yours. Heal it. Ignorance is yours. Banish it. War is yours. Stop it. Hope is yours. Confirm it. America is yours. Save it. The world is yours. Serve it. The dream is yours. Claim it.
>
> Don't be blinded by prejudice, disheartened by the times, or discouraged by the system. Face the system. Challenge it. Change it. Confront it. Correct it. Don't let anything paralyze your mind, tie your hands, or defeat your spirit. Take the world, not to dominate it, but to deliver it. Not to exploit it, but to enrich it. Take the dream and inherit the earth.

In short, use your wisdom, your learning and your influence to change the world and leave it better than you found it. That is why you're on this journey. That is why you are in The Pursuit.

A Gift from Karyn

Something happened in my life while I was completing this book, and I just had to tell you about it. In "Principle Three: Pay Your Dues," I talked about my daughter Karyn and her dream of pursuing a music career. Just days after that chapter was written, Karyn told me that she had resigned her job in Orlando and was moving to Nashville. She's launching out in The Pursuit—she's pursuing her dreams—this time as a mature and focused young woman who is willing to pay her dues.

Karyn left Florida on July 17, 2007, and the night before her departure, we went out for a farewell dinner at McCormick and Schmick's. We had many laughs over dinner, and yes, a few tears. But I could see by the sparkle in her eyes that she was launching out with a sense of adventure.

I gave Karyn a farewell gift, and she said, "Thank you, Daddy—and I have something for you." She gave me a framed picture of the two of us together, which now graces my desk. And along with the picture was a card that she had written. It was a thank-you note for the influence I've had on her life. My vision blurred as I read these words:

Daddy—

On one of my flights to Philadelphia, I was overcome with the urge to get out a piece of paper and write down everything that I've learned from you. Here's what I came up with:

1. Wear your seatbelt.
2. Enjoy your life.
3. Be good to people.
4. Life is about relationships and collecting friends.
5. Work hard every day.
6. Take care of your body.
7. Exercise your mind.
8. Dare to live big.
9. Never stop building your résumé.
10. There are no giants out there.
11. The world will take care of the jerks.
12. Make good decisions.
13. You can't quit—it's a league rule.
14. Stay close to the Lord—He's with you on the mountains as well as in the valleys.

So, Dad, as I'm embarking on this very exciting but very scary journey, I want to thank you for everything you have taught me. I am the person I am today because of the example you set for me. I feel prepared to go out and fight for what I want because you taught me to believe in myself. I love you more than life itself, and I am SO proud to be your daughter.

Now it's time for me to go and make you proud!!!

I love you!
Karyn

Somehow, I felt sure that Mr. Littlejohn was reading over my shoulder—and he was smiling.

Endnotes

1. Control What You Can

1. Author uncredited, "Examining the Dynamics of Control—Author Viorst Looks at Our Struggles with Power and Surrender," originally published in the *Seattle Times*, 1998, retrieved at http://www.iconocast.com/News_Files/ZZZNewsN7_XX/News7.htm.
2. Ron Willingham, *The People Principle: A Revolutionary Redefinition of Leadership* (New York: St. Martin's Griffin, 1999), p. 169.
3. Brian Tracy, *Goals: How to Get Everything You Want Faster Than You Ever Thought Possible* (San Francisco: Berrett-Koehler Publishers, 2004), p. 23.
4. Dean Smith with Gerald D. Bell and John Kilgo, *Carolina Way: Leadership Lessons from a Life in Coaching* (New York: Penguin, 2005), p. 30.
5. John Stossel, *20/20*, ABC television network, September 20, 1998.

2. Be Patient

1. Bethany McLean and Peter Elkind, *Smartest Guys in the Room: The Amazing Rise and Scandalous Fall of Enron* (New York: Penguin, 2003), p. 137.
2. Brad Foss, "The man behind Enron's infamous partnerships," Associated Press wire story, February 6, 2002.
3. Tom Fowler, "Enron's implosion was anything but sudden," *The Houston Chronicle*, December 20, 2005, retrieved at http://www.chron.com/disp/story.mpl/special/enron/2655409.html.
4. Harvey B. Mackay, *Swim with the Sharks Without Being Eaten Alive* (New York: William Morrow and Company, Inc., 1988), n.p.
5. John Wooden with Jay Carty, *Coach Wooden's Pyramid of Success: Building Blocks for a Better Life* (Ventura, CA: Regal Books: 2005), p. 126.
6. Mark H. McCormick, *Never Wrestle with a Pig and Ninety Other Ideas to Build Your Business and Career* (New York: Penguin Books: 2002), p. 123.

3. Pay Your Dues

1. Maria Shriver, *Ten Things I Wish I'd Known Before I Went Out into the Real World* (New York: Grand Central Publishing, 2000), p. 21.
2. Laura Ziv, "Life isn't going exactly as planned? Get over it!" *Cosmopolitan*, March 1, 1998, p. 28.
3. Shriver, *Ten Things I Wish I'd Known Before I Went Out into the Real World*, n.p.

4. Keep It Simple

1. Quoted by Michael Warshaw, "Keep It Simple," *Fast Company*, June 1, 1998, p. 154.
2. Quoted by Colleen O'Connor, "Simplicity Pattern," *The Dallas Morning News*, August 13, 1998, p. 1C.
3. Quoted by Jim Jones, "Simplicity Trend Gains Momentum," *Minneapolis Star Tribune*, November 12, 1997, p. 9E.

4. Karl Ruegg, "Coaching tip: Look for simple solutions," adapted from "Step-By-Step Success" by Lorraine Ash, retrieved at http://topten.org/public/AP/AP85.html.

5. David Anderson, Chairman of Famous Dave's, interview with Ann Sundius, MSNBC Business, 10 September 1997; Press Release, December 15, 2003: "Famous Dave's of America Announces Senate Confirmation of David Anderson as Assistant Secretary of the Interior, Indian Affairs"; Famous Dave's, Dave Anderson Biography, retrieved at http://www.famousdaves.com/biograph.cfm.

6. Quoted by Tom Timmermann, "Timeouts Are Coaches' Time In with Players," *St. Louis Post-Dispatch*, March 22, 1998, p. F3.

7. Quoted in "Upstarts blazed a similar trail," *USA Today*, Wednesday, April 25, 2007, p. 3C.

8. Timmermann, "Timeouts Are Coaches' Time In with Players."

9. Warshaw, "Keep It Simple."

5. Don't Run from Your Problems

1. Joseph Conrad, "Typhoon," *Typhoon and Other Tales, rev. ed.* (Oxford, England: Oxford University Press, 2002), n.p.

2. Brian Tracy, *Change Your Thinking, Change Your Life: How to Unlock Your Full Potential for Success and Achievement* (Hoboken, NJ: Wiley, 2003), pp. 159-160.

3. Walter Anderson, *The Confidence Course: Sevens Steps to Self-Fulfillment* (New York: Harper, 1998), p. 18.

4. Colin Powell, quoted by Peter Benesh, "Powell on Soldiers and Trust," *Investor's Business Daily*, February 13, 2007, retrieved at http://www.investors.com/editorial/IBDArticles.asp?artsec=21&issue=20070212.

5. M. Scott Peck, *The Road Less Traveled, 25th Anniversary Edition: A New Psychology of Love, Traditional Values and Spiritual Growth* (New York: Touchstone, 2003), p. 3.

6. Rick Warren, "Developing your creativity for ministry," Rick Warren's Ministry Toolbox, retrieved at http://www.pastors.com/RWMT/default.asp?id=116&artid=3250&expand=1.

7. Doug Hall, *Jump Start Your Brain* (New York: Grand Central Publishing, 1996), pp. 59-60.

6. Pay Attention to the Little Things

1. Paul S. Goldner, *Red-Hot Cold Call Selling* (New York: American Management Association, 2nd edition, 2006), p. 8.

2. Whitey Herzog, *You're Missin' a Great Game* (New York: Berkley, 2000), pp. 8-9.

3. Oren Harari, *The Leadership Secrets of Colin Powell* (New York: McGraw-Hill, 2002), p. 148.

4. Quoted in "Rupert Murdoch Quotes," ThinkExist.com, retrieved at http://thinkexist.com/quotes/rupert_murdoch/.
5. Zig Ziglar, *Courtship After Marriage* (Nashville, TN: Thomas Nelson, 1993), p. 93.
6. Ibid.
7. Og Mandino, *The Spellbinder's Gift* (New York: Ballantine, 1996), p. 193. Emphasis in the original.
8. Bernie Brillstein, *The Little Stuff Matters Most* (New York: Gotham/Penguin, 2004), p. xii.
9. Jennifer Rothschild, "Not Enough Time," WomensMinistry.Net eNewsletter, May 10, 2006, retrieved at http://www.womensministry.net/Newsletter_New/WomensMinistry.Net%20Issue%20313.htm.
10. Ronald Reagan, *An American Life* (New York: Simon & Schuster, 1990), p. 19.
11. James L. Garlow, *The 21 Irrefutable Laws of Leadership—Tested by Time* (Nashville, TN: Thomas Nelson, 2002), p. 44.
12. "Favorite Quotations—Zig Ziglar," DailyCelebrations.com, retrieved at http://www.dailycelebrations.com/zig2.htm.

7. The Pursuit of Wisdom

1. Eugene Peterson, *The Message Remix* (Colorado Springs, CO: NavPress), p. 2198.
2. Stephen S. Hall, "The Older-and-Wiser Hypothesis," *The New York Times*, May 6, 2007, retrieved at http://www.nytimes.com/2007/05/06/magazine/06Wisdom-t.html?pagewanted=1&ei=5088&en=4b4959cf047f61fe&ex=1336104000&partner=rssnyt&emc=rss.
3. Ibid.
4. Russell Sullivan, *Rocky Marciano: The Rock of His Times* (Urbana and Chicago, IL: University of Illinois Press, 2002), p. 270.

8. The Mindset of a Learner

1. Quoted by Glenn Rymsza, Catholic Student Association at Portland State University, retrieved at http://www.csa.pdx.edu/.
2. Celia Sandys with Jonathan Littman, *We Shall Not Fail: The Inspiring Leadership of Winston Churchill* (New York: Penguin, 2003), p. 159.
3. Brian Tracy, "Three Skills to Improve Conversation," Brian Tracy's Blog, May 14, 2007, retrieved at http://blogs.briantracy.com/public/blog/169064.
4. Anna Quindlen, "Still the Brightest," *Newsweek*, May 14, 2007, retrieved at http://today.msnbc.msn.com/id/18507630/site/newsweek/.
5. William Lyon Phelps, "The Pleasure of Books," radio address, April 6, 1933, retrieved at http://www.historyplace.com/speeches/phelps.htm.
6. Charles McGrath, "Most Valuable Player," *New York Times Magazine*, 1996, retrieved at http://www.nytimes.com/specials/magazine4/articles/zaharias.html.
7. Pat Jordan, quoted in Phil Rizzuto and Tom Horton, *The October Twelve: Five Years of Yankee Glory 1949-1953* (New York: Forge Books, 1994), p. 77.

Acknowledgments

With deep appreciation I acknowledge the support and guidance of the following people who helped make this book possible:

Special thanks to Bob Vander Weide, Rich DeVos and Alex Martins of the Orlando Magic.

Hats off to five associates—my assistants Andrew Herdliska and Latria Graham, my adviser Ken Hussar, Jason McFerren of the Orlando Magic mail/copy room, and my ace typist Fran Thomas.

I also want to express deep gratitude to Bill Greig III, Kim Bangs, Steven Lawson and Mark Weising of Regal Publishing Group, and to my partner in writing this book, Jim Denney. Thank you for believing that we had something important to say.

And, finally, special thanks and appreciation go to my wife, Ruth, and to my wonderful and supportive family. They are truly the backbone of my life.

Contact Information

You can contact Pat Williams at:

Pat Williams
c/o Orlando Magic
8701 Maitland Summit Boulevard
Orlando, FL 32810
phone: (407) 916-2404
pwilliams@orlandomagic.com

Visit Pat Williams's website at:

www.PatWilliamsMotivate.com

If you would like to set up a speaking engagement
for Pat Williams, please call or write his assistant,
Andrew Herdliska, at the above address or call him at
407-916-2401. Requests can also be faxed to 407-916-2986
or emailed to aherdliska@orlandomagic.com.
We would love to hear from you. Please send your comments about this book to Pat Williams at the above
address or in care of our publisher at the address below.
Thank you.

Pat Williams
c/o Regal Publishing Group
1957 Eastman Ave.
Ventura, California 93003

MORE GREAT RESOURCES FROM
REGAL

The Warrior Within
Becoming Complete in the Four
Crucial Dimensions of Manhood
Pat Williams & Jim Denney
ISBN 978.08307.39028

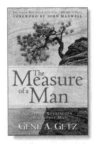

The Measure of a Man
Twenty Attributes of a Godly Man
Gene A. Getz
ISBN 978.08307.34955

Breakfast with Fred
Fred Smith
ISBN 978.08307.44763

The Seven Rules of Success
Indispensable Wisdom for Successful Living
Wayne Cordeiro
ISBN 978.08307.42943